PINE POINT
HIGHWAY TO THE SEA
DUXBURY BEACH
Wm. J. Wright
HIGH PINES
Wm. J. Wright
URY
PLYMOUTH
CLARKS ISLAND
W.H.Watson
J.M.Watson
W.Watson
J. Deacon
E.W.Watson
PLUM HILLS
SAQUISH NECK
A.A.Gilson
YE GURNET INN (1752)
J.L.Boardman
L.S.Sta.
Mrs.J.P.Holmes
GURNET
TWIN LIGHT
S.P.Burgess
J.P.Thurber
SAQUISH HEAD
Back River
Powder Pt
Duxbury Beach
High Pines
High Pine Ledge
Clarks Island
Saquish Neck
Saquish Head
Fort Standish
Gurnet Pt
ANNUAL DECREASE

The DUXBURY BEACH *Book*

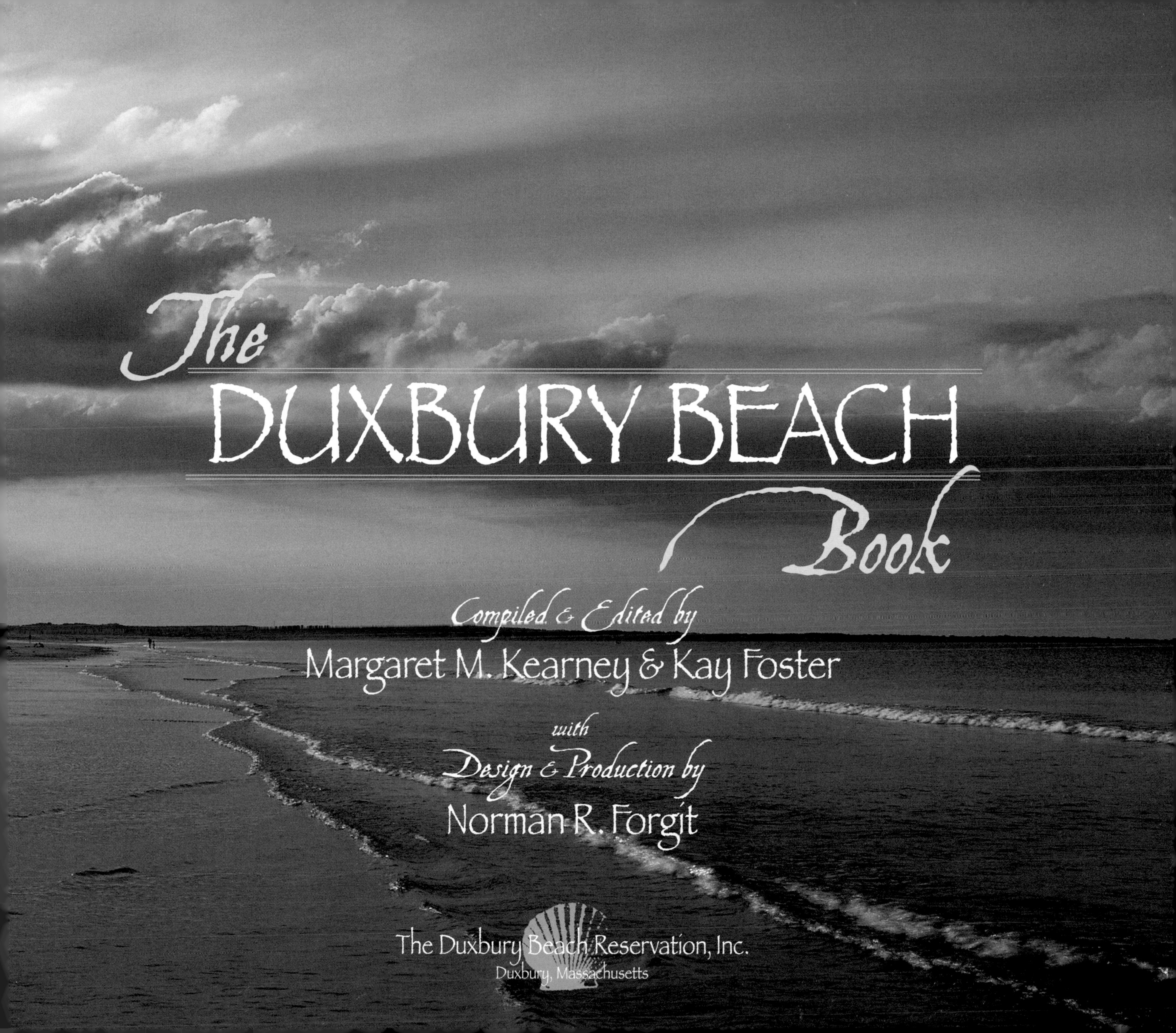

The DUXBURY BEACH *Book*

Compiled & Edited by

Margaret M. Kearney & Kay Foster

with

Design & Production by

Norman R. Forgit

The Duxbury Beach Reservation, Inc.
Duxbury, Massachusetts

Printed in the United States of America
ISBN-10: 0-9793411-0-8
ISBN-13: 978-0-9793411-0-6

First Edition
5 4 3 2

Table of Contents

To the memory of Frederick S. Pratt (1873 – 1968), without whom the story of Duxbury Beach would have been much different.

Preface

As anyone who has been to Duxbury Beach knows, it is a place of beauty. It is also a place that has given rise to an untold number of stories—stories about its creation, about the storms that have threatened it, about the birds and animals that have sought shelter and food from it, and about the people who have lived on it, played on it, and worked to protect it from both natural and human threats.

Many of these stories have been handed down by word of mouth through the generations, have been written about in various newspaper and magazine articles, and have been the subject of paintings and photographs by amateurs and renowned professionals alike. But until now, they have never been collected and published in one place. *The Duxbury Beach Book* is the first book to compile the stories of the beach, from its formation to present-day efforts to preserve it for future generations. It is a publication of the Duxbury Beach Reservation, Inc., the nonprofit organization that owns the beach.

The design and layout of the book are the work of Norman R. Forgit. Norman is well known for his publications in conjunction with the Duxbury Rural & Historical Society. A summer resident of Saquish, Norman contributed many of the photographs he has taken of the beach over the years.

The Duxbury Beach Book begins with the geological story of the beach, told by Jim O'Connell, a coastal geologist for the Woods Hole Oceanographic Institution's Sea Grant Program and a trustee of the Reservation. In Chapter 2, Ducky Kelso, author of *Old Colony Wildflowers*, provides a whimsical description of the still-familiar plants, insects, and clams that the pilgrims encountered almost 400 years ago. Local historian Tony Kelso describes in Chapter 3 the period from the arrival of the Pilgrims through the late 1800s when people began to see the commercial potential of the beach. In Chapter 4, Al Krahmer, the Reservation trustee who master-minded unprecedented beach repairs twice in recent history, writes about three of the devastating storms that have struck Duxbury Beach.

No book about the beach would be complete without the story of the original Powder Point Bridge and its reconstruction one hundred years later. Margaret Kearney, a Reservation trustee and member of the bridge reconstruction committee, covers these historic structures in Chapter 5. For Chapter 6, Kay Foster, another Reservation trustee, researched volumes of Duxbury Beach Association records to tell how a few individuals put a stop to development plans by buying the beach in 1919, preserved it in its natural state, and then turned it over to the Duxbury Beach Reservation in 1975. Kay also wrote the last chapter, which describes the Reservation's current management practices and its partnership with the town of Duxbury.

At the southernmost end of Duxbury Beach are the Gurnet and Saquish, which along with Clark's Island are part of Plymouth. Most people who live in these places are summer residents, although a few hardy souls like Elaine Nudd are year-round residents. Elaine, who lives on the Gurnet and is a trustee of the Reservation, shares historical glimpses of the Gurnet, Saquish, and Clark's Island in Chapter 7. Elaine also contributed most of the historical photos of the Gurnet and Saquish.

The seasonal rhythms of migratory birds and other beach creatures are described in Chapter 8, written by David Clapp, the recently retired southeast regional director of Mass Audubon and currently a wildlife consultant. Wildlife photographer Shawn Carey of Migration Productions donated many of the spectacular photographs in this chapter.

The cover photograph is by Mike Sleeper, who is very well known for his beachscapes. Some of the chapter-opening photos are also Mike Sleeper's. Jason Wolfson, a trustee of the Reservation, took many of the aerial photographs that appear in the book. Scott Hecker, director of the National Audubon Society's Coastal Bird Conservation program, donated photographs of piping plovers. Many other people also donated photographs, and all are listed in the photo credits on pages x and xi.

Patrick Browne, executive director of the Duxbury Rural & Historical Society, was most supportive, giving us access to the society's records and archives and answering many of our questions. He also wrote the side bar on Sarah Wingate Taylor. William "Skip" Taylor and Clint Watson, both of whom are descendents of the original Watsons of Clark's Island and still have summer homes on the island, provided insights into its history. Skip also gave us photographs and memorabilia of his aunt, Sarah Wingate Taylor.

Others on the Book Committee worked tirelessly on different aspects of the book. Nancy Bennett and Norman Tucker deserve special recognition for the hours they spent poring over collections of old books and photographs. John Nash, Dick Whitney, Noreen Wenger, and Arthur Evans contributed valuable suggestions and support. Sarah Evans and William Kearney, Jr. provided excellent editorial assistance. Margaret Kearney conceived the project, gathered the group, and kept everyone focused for over two years.

Proceeds from the sale of *The Duxbury Beach Book* will support the efforts of Duxbury Beach Reservation, Inc., to preserve the beach. The Duxbury Beach Preservation Society, the educational and fund-raising subcommittee of the Reservation, underwrote publication and is handling marketing and distribution of the book.

Photo Credits

The following is a list of those who supplied images for this book, along with the pages* on which the images appear.

Frederick D. Atwood: *137 b*

Dot & Dan Baker: *52 b; 54; 55 b*

Mary Barclay: *48; 58*

Nancy and Bill Bennett: *31; 103; 122 c*

Mrs. Ralph (Thelma) Blakeman:
88; 89; 90

Shawn P. Carey
(Migration Productions):
iv; 68; 128; 130 r; 135 b; 136; 137 t, c; 138; 139; 140; 141; 142; 143 t; 145 b

Margaret S. Connors: *19 r; 21 t*

Duxbury Rural & Historical Society:
10 (inset); 22 (inset); 29; 30 t; 33 l; 35; 37 b; 39; 40 t; 42; 43; 44 (inset); 51 t; 52 t; 60 t; 73; 74; 75 t; 105; 111; 112 b; 118 b; 124; 125 t; 127 b

Norman R. Forgit: *Back Cover (inset 1&3); i; vi; viii; x; xii; 4; 6; 8; 10; 12; 14; 16; 18; 19 t, b; 20; 21 b; 22; 24; 26; 28; 30 b; 32; 33 r; 34; 39 b; 44; 60 b; 64 b; 66; 70; 72 b; 80; 82; 84; 86 l; 94 b; 96 b; 98; 99; 100; 101; 102 b; 104 b; 106; 108; 110; 116 b; 119 t, c; 120 t; 120 b; 130 l; 132; 134; 135 t; 143 b; 146; 148; 150 b; 166; 168; 170; 172*

* *t = top; c = center; b = bottom; l = left; r = right.*

Joe Grady: *62*

Scott S. Hecker: *144; 145 t*

The family of Jim Kelso: *65*

Al Krahmer: *63; 64 t; 69; 71; 72 t; 76 t; 77*

Mrs. Robert G. Millar: *38 b; 41; 51 b*

John Nash: *47; 76 b*

Elaine M. Nudd: *37 t; 38 t; 38 c; 94 t; 95; 96 t; 102 t; 112 t; 113; 114; 115; 116 t; 117; 118 t; 119 b; 120 c; 121 t; 122 t, b; 152; 156*

Jim O'Connell: *5; 8 t; 150 t; 164*

Barbara Peavey: *107*

Katherine Pillsbury: *25*

Nina Pratt: vi

Collection of Walter Prince: *86 r; 104 t*

Mike Sleeper: *Cover; Back Cover (inset 4); ii; iii; 56; 78; 92*

Fred Stetson: *46; 50; 154*

William Watson Taylor, Jr.: *40 b; 75 b; 123; 125 b, c; 126; 127 t*

Jason Wolfson: *Back Cover (inset 2); 2; 6 t; 121 b; 157; 158; 159; 160; 161; 162*

The DUXBURY BEACH Book

1 Duxbury Beach... The Beginning

A Geological View of the Beach

Duxbury Beach is one of the few long stretches of sandy shore between Boston and Cape Cod. It extends from Marshfield in the north to Gurnet Point in the south, a distance of about 6 miles. Separated from the mainland by Duxbury Bay, it is a barrier beach, and together with Long Beach in Plymouth, it protects the waterfront areas of Duxbury, Kingston, and Plymouth from storm waves and flooding. It is flanked on both the ocean and inland sides by wide, expansive tidal flats, and on its inland side are highly productive salt marshes and meandering tidal creeks.

The beach as we know it today—a narrow, low-lying strip of sand, pebble, cobble, and grassy dunes—began forming about 4,000 years ago. It is the product of a rising sea level and the erosion of glacial landforms. Over time, various forces—among them, a continuing rise in sea level, overwashes from storms, and temporary tidal inlets created by storms—have caused the beach to migrate about half a mile inland to its present position, which, at the closest point, is about half a mile from the mainland.

Aerial view looking south showing Duxbury Beach, Gurnet Point, Saquish Beach, and Clark's Island.

Timeline

18-13,000 B.C. 2000 B.C.

18-13,000 B.C. – Glacial deposits form headlands/drumlins at the southern end of Gurnet Road, the Gurnet, Saquish Head, and Clark's Island.

2000 B.C. – Sediments eroding from glacial headlands begin forming Duxbury Beach.

At right is a graphic showing an evolutionary model of the landward migration of Duxbury Beach (modified from Hill & Fitzgerald, 1992).

Geologists predict that the beach will continue its landward migration and that it may one day weld itself onto the Duxbury mainland.

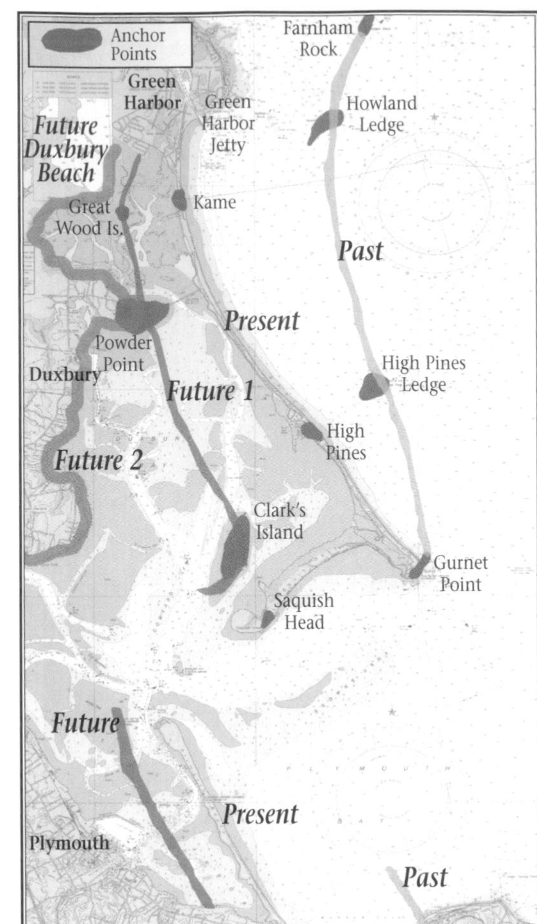

Evolution

To understand how Duxbury Beach evolved, we have to go back some 20,000 years, to the final stage of the last Ice Age known as the Wisconsin. During that stage, the glacier reached its southernmost point, creating the northern hills of Nantucket and Martha's Vineyard. As it moved south, the glacier scraped and pulled along with it the silt, sand, cobble, and boulders from the landmasses over which it passed in what is now Canada and northern New England. It was a sheet of ice, possibly a mile high.

By approximately 15,000 years ago, the climate had warmed, and the glacier had melted and retreated north to the present position of Duxbury, Kingston, and Plymouth Bays. As it melted, it left behind the material it had collected on its journey south. These deposits formed the present ground surface of Duxbury and surrounding towns. They also formed the three headlands to which Duxbury Beach is now anchored.

At its northern end, Duxbury Beach is attached to a jetty at Green Harbor, and just beyond that, to the south, is a waterfront area of single-family homes protected by a concrete seawall. South of that are the three anchoring points for the barrier beach. The first is a kame—a small, circular hill of glacial drift—at the southern boundary of Marshfield. Like the waterfront just south of Green Harbor, this section of the beach is densely populated and protected by a seawall. The next anchor is at the northern edge of High Pines, a relatively deserted area about a mile south of the Powder Point Bridge. Although large, wind-blown sand dunes cover the surface of High Pines, the underlying layers consist of glacial till deposited 15,000 to 20,000 years ago. The southernmost anchor is the drumlin (an elongated hill of glacial till) of Gurnet Point, which is today a small community clustered around a historic lighthouse.

The seawall along the northern portion of the barrier beach.

Extending west from Gurnet Point is Saquish Neck, a small barrier beach with several lines of coastal dunes, backed by an expansive salt marsh and meandering tidal creeks. It is attached to Saquish Head, another drumlin deposited under the mile-high glacial ice sheet 15,000 to 20,000 years ago. Yet another reminder of glacial activity in Duxbury Bay is the drumlin of Clark's Island.

The retreating glacier created many other elevated landforms that are still visible today, among them the backbone of Cape Cod (upon which Route 6, the Cape's central highway, was constructed), the high bluffs of southern Plymouth, Captain's Hill in Duxbury, and the spectacular shoreline cliffs in Scituate. The sea covered and eroded an untold number of similar landforms long ago, some offshore of Duxbury Beach. The erosion of these offshore landforms was a primary source of the sediment that later helped form the beach.

Long before Duxbury Beach was formed, the melting glacier created several large freshwater lakes, notably Glacial Lake Cape Cod (which was some 65 feet higher than Cape Cod Bay is today) and, west of that, Glacial Lake Taunton. After the Cape Cod Bay ice lobe moved north of the Duxbury area, Glacial Lake Taunton catastrophically drained down a lowland toward what became Duxbury, Kingston, and Plymouth Bays. The drainage carved out what is now the 40- to 70-foot-deep entrance channel to those bays.

Before the glacier began its retreat north, the sea level was some 300 feet lower than it is today, and the shoreline was approximately 90 miles south of Nantucket and a couple of hundred miles east of where it is now, beyond George's Bank. As the glacier melted, the sea level began to rise, causing the shoreline to recede. Waves and tides gradually eroded offshore glacial landforms and washed the eroded material along the shore, where it formed temporary barriers, sand sheets, and flood-tide deltas.

Timeline

1500 B.C. 1000 A.D. 1400 A.D.

1500 B.C. – Duxbury Beach is located 1,600 feet east of its present position.

1000 A.D. – Vikings explore from Newfoundland to Cape Cod.

1400 A.D. – Duxbury Beach is located 500 feet east of its present position.

This aerial photo of Gurnet Point shows Duxbury Beach (at right) and Saquish Beach (at left) separated by salt marshes and meandering tidal creeks.

When the rate of sea-level rise slowed about 3,500 to 4,000 years ago, so did the landward movement of offshore sediment. These deposits of sand and gravel began to accumulate. The supply of offshore sediment was augmented by material eroded from onshore drumlins like Gurnet Point, which was at the time much larger and extended farther seaward. Sediment from eroding landforms to the north (present-day Marshfield and Scituate) added to the supply. During this stage, sand spits began to protrude from the glacial headlands that today anchor Duxbury Beach, and they eventually joined together to form the present configuration of the shoreline.

Peat that has occasionally surfaced in front of the Duxbury Beach pavilion and other areas along the beach after severe storms has provided interesting evidence of the beach's landward migration. Peat is the partially carbonized substrate through which salt marsh grows, and its presence on the seaward side of the beach indicates that this area was once a salt marsh and that the beach was located farther to the east. In its landward migration, the barrier beach has actually been rolling over itself in response to storm overwash, temporary inlet formation, and a rising sea level.

Shoreline Change

Today, storm waves and tidal energy are the main forces that control the form and shoreline position of Duxbury Beach. However, human activity over the past century has also had a significant impact.

Historically, a primary source of sand and pebble for Duxbury Beach has been erosion of the Scituate and Marshfield shoreline. Storm-induced currents transported these materials south and deposited them on Duxbury Beach. Because of extensive armoring of most of the Scituate and Marshfield shoreline with seawalls to protect shoreline development, the sediments that once fed Duxbury Beach (as well as the beaches of Scituate and Marshfield) have significantly diminished. Less sand is now reaching Duxbury Beach, leaving cobble exposed for more extended times during the year.

Since the mid-1800s, the U.S. Coast Survey (now the National Ocean Service) has been plotting the position of high water around the United States. Data for Duxbury Beach show that in the vicinity of the Powder Point Bridge, the high water line has moved inland about 300 feet since the mid-1800s and that the rate of erosion since the 1950s has

Carbon Dating the Age of Duxbury Beach

All living organisms contain the same ratio of carbon 12 to carbon 14 atoms. This ratio remains constant until death, at which point carbon 14 atoms begin to decay. The number of carbon 12 atoms, however, remains the same after death. Because scientists know the decaying rate of carbon 14, they can measure the ratio between it and carbon 12 to determine the age of deceased plants and animals.

The analyses of two peat deposits by geologists from Boston University have established radiocarbon dates that tell us more about the formation of Duxbury Beach. A radiocarbon age of 3,700 years B.P. (before the present) of peat collected from 13 feet below the salt marsh on the inland side of the beach, together with data showing that mean sea level at this time was 18 feet below present sea level, indicates that the beach was then positioned approximately 1,600 feet offshore. Analysis of the other peat deposit, which was taken from in front of the Duxbury Beach pavilion, suggests that the shoreline 588 years ago was at least 500 feet seaward of where it is today.

Timeline

1603

1605

1614

1603 – Martin Pring explores the coast from Maine to Cape Cod.

1605 – Samuel de Champlain maps Plymouth Bay from Manomet to the Gurnet, showing Saquish and Clark's Island.

1614 – Captain John Smith explores New England and creates a map the later colonists used.

Exposed peat in front of the Duxbury Beach pavilion after the October 1991 No-Name Storm. This peat and the salt marsh that once grew from it formed thousands of years ago when Duxbury Beach was seaward of the deposit.

accelerated. These data also show that the beach in this area has narrowed from approximately 460 feet in the mid-1800s to 210 feet in the 1990s. The narrowing is the result of both the reduction in sediment supply and continuing sea-level rise and storms.

In the area between High Pines and Plum Hills, the beach has not eroded as much. The high-water line since the mid-1800s has moved landward approximately 125 feet, and the width of the beach has narrowed from about 292 feet in the mid-1800s to 170 feet in the mid-1990s. The main reason that this area of the beach is eroding at a slower rate than areas to the north is the offshore presence of High Pines Ledge. The ledge not only reduces storm wave energy; it also deflects northeast storm waves in such a way that it creates a current that travels from Gurnet Point north to High Pines. This current converges with a southward flowing current in the vicinity of High Pines. When the two currents meet, they deposit the sand, pebble, and gravel they are carrying, resulting in a slower erosion rate. That is why there is more sand and higher dunes along this part of the shore.

The Future

Recent documentation shows that Duxbury Beach is migrating landward at approximately one foot per year, and that rate may increase as the rate of sea-level rise accelerates and more major storms

Documenting Movement of the Beach

In 1998 the Duxbury Beach Reservation began to record the width and height of the beach on a regular basis in order to document the changes that occur in this dynamic environment. To do so, it hired coastal geology consultants who chose eight locations to take the measurements. The spots were selected to represent various widths, substrates, and human uses of the beach.

At each of these sites, a 16-foot long stainless steel rod was buried 15 feet deep, leaving about 1 foot above the surface of the sand. A higher wooden post also was erected next to each rod to help geologists find them. The rods are so long that if another catastrophic storm damages the beach, they can still be found. The exact coordinates and elevation of the top of each rod have been recorded as well. The rods are numbered from north to south, with the first situated in the pavilion parking lot and the last in the Plum Hills area at the southern end of the beach.

The rods enable both horizontal and vertical measurements from the low-water mark on the ocean side to the low-water mark on the bay side. Twice a year, geologists plot the data and produce a side view, or profile, of the beach at each location. Over several years of data collection, the Reservation can analyze the movement of Duxbury Beach and other environmental changes.

wash over the dunes. Geologists predict that the southern end of the beach will eventually detach from Gurnet Point, turning Gurnet Point into Gurnet Island. Continuing its migration, the beach will weld onto Clark's Island, changing Clark's Island into Clark's Point sometime in the not-too-distant geologic future. It may then detach from Clark's Island and ultimately weld onto the Duxbury mainland, turning Clark's Island into an island once again. In its travels landward, the beach will fill existing tidal and navigation channels, create more sand flats and shoals in Duxbury Bay, and ultimately form a wide, sandy beach along the mainland. Duxbury Beach will have changed its form—from a barrier beach to a mainland beach. The Duxbury waterfront will then be exposed to the full fury of storm waves, but it will also have miles of sandy beach and dramatic ocean views.

Timeline

1620

1636

December 8-9, 1620 – Exploring party from the *Mayflower* escapes treacherous rocks on the Gurnet and Saquish and lands on Clark's Island.

December 16, 1620 – *Mayflower* sails into Plymouth Harbor.

1636 – Cut River Canal is dug to provide safe boat passage from Duxbury Bay to Green Harbor.

Port St Louis

2 Duxbury Beach… A Most Excellent Place

Discovering Natural Wonders

Duxbury Beach can be seen in the map that French explorer Samuel de Champlain drew in 1605. His ship grounded on the "shallow shore," and while he waited for the tide to come in, he recorded his observations of this "Most Excellent Place." Champlain's eye was caught by some of the curiosities of the bay. For example, here is his description of the horseshoe crab:

> *The length of the tail varies according to their size. With the end of it [the native people] pointed their arrows, and it contains also a row of prickles like the large shell in which are their eyes. There are eight small feet . . . and two behind longer and flatter, which they use in swimming. There are also in front two other very small ones with which they eat. Under the small shell there are membranes which swell up, and beat like the throat of a frog, and rest upon each other like the folds of a waistcoat. The largest specimen of this fish that I saw was a foot broad and a foot and a half long.*[1]

Bayside colonies of blue asters foretell autumn. Inset: The French explorer Samuel de Champlain mapped his impressions of Duxbury Bay in 1605.

Timeline

1637 1638 1644 1656

1637 – Duxbury is incorporated as a town.

1638 – Gurnet, Saquish, and Clark's Island are granted to Plymouth.

1644 – Death of Elder William Brewster.

1656 – Death of Myles Standish.

Abundance

When the first European settlers entered the bay in 1620, "winding in compass like a snaile," they were astounded. Pinched and hungry from a long, risky voyage, they came upon a rich banquet. In the sheltered waters, deeper then than now, was all the cod they could eat and enough also "to lade" their vessels. There were "blewfish," a new tasty treat, and bass, enormous and plentiful, especially in Duxbury "crike" [creek]. Here, too, they found eels; "in September we can take a hogshead of eels in a night," Pilgrim Edward Winslow wrote a friend in England.[2]

William Wood, in 1634, described oysters "shaped like a shoehorn," and clams (or "clamps") would be eaten more often were it not "for better fish: A man running over the clam banks will presently be made all wet by their spouting of water."[3]

Early explorers, usually arriving in summer, exulted in all sorts of sweet fruits and berries—some familiar, some not. Martin Pring, who had noted the snail-shaped bay, mentions strawberries, "very fair and big," covering the sandy, sunny shore of Saquish. There were at least three kinds of plums, one "almost as good as damsons" in the opinion of Edward Winslow. Beach plums were not an immediate success, although an early document indicates that Native Americans valued them highly. One chief sold his lands to a colonist but reserved "all liberty and privileges of plumming."[4]

The great diversity of birds—especially game birds—intrigued the newcomers. The possibilities for food ranked high. Turkeys "that ran as fast as a dog" would in winter resort to the seashore to look "for shrimp and such small fishes at low tide."[5]

John Josselyn's 1672 best seller reports "sanderlins," in flocks. "They are about the bigness of a Sparrow, and in the fall of the leaf will be all fat; when I was first in the Countrie (i.e., c. 1638) the English cut them into small pieces to put into the Pudding instead of suet. I have known twelve-score and above kill'd at two shots."[6]

Cranes (possibly herons) had rather dubious potential for food. William Wood observed that although the bird was almost as tall as a man "by reason of his long legs and neck, yet is his body rounder than other fowls, yet did I never see one that was fat—though very sleeky . . . of these there be many; in summer but none in winter. Their price is two shillings."[7]

Clearly, the colonists were taking note of seasonal changes but not entirely with understanding. Josselyn thought the "humbird" slept all winter so "was not seen until spring."[8] Bass and "blewfish" would sometimes disappear in a most puzzling way, and the eels in the creeks' marshy grasses buried themselves in winter deep in the icy mud.

At home, the English had already been alerted to erosion control by the Elizabethan government. Here, they soon recognized the staying power of beach grasses. After the arrival of cattle, the use of grasslands became a major issue.

By now, the settlers also recognized some drawbacks to the Eden. Josselyn wrote:

> *The Sea Coasts are accounted wholesome, the East and South Wind as coming from the Sea produceth warm weather, the Northwest coming over land causeth extremity of cold, and many times strikes the Inhabitants both English and Indian with that sad Disease called there the Plague of the Back . . .*[9]

Nor were all the "rarities" beneficial. The "Squnck" had urine "of so strong a scent that if it light upon anything there's no abiding of it."[10] "Jaccals" (coyotes) were seen in our area but not rattlesnakes. Butterflies, though "diverse," earned scarcely a mention. The greatest "pesterments" were insects:

> *The Countrey is strangely incommodated with flyes, which the English call Musketaes . . . they will sting so fiercely*

No More Featherbeds from Waterfowl

Justin Winsor, in his ***History of the Town of Duxbury*** (1849), p. 27, writes of the loss of water fowl:

The bay has been, from the earliest times a resort of wild sea fowl of every kind, which has often drawn hither crowds of sportsmen. And as early as 1737, the town, through fear of the total destruction of the game, voted to petition the General Court to regulate the fowling, "because ye wild fowle have almost forsaken ye said bay . . . Few now can boast of . . . having by his gun furnished materials for eight featherbeds."

Timeline

1657 – Death of William Bradford, author of *History of Plimoth Plantation, 1620-1647*.

1662 – Death of Massasoit.

1672 – John Josselyn writes *New-Englands Rarities Discovered*, a work much admired by Thoreau.

in summer as to make the faces of the English swell'd and scabby, as if the small pox for the first year. Likewise there is a small black fly no bigger than a flea . . . . There is another sort of fly called a Gurnipper that are like our horse-flyes, and will bite desperately, making the bloud to spurt out in great quantity; these trouble our English cattle very much, raising swellings as big as an egg in their hides. . . . Likewise there be infinite numbers of Tikes [ticks] hanging upon the bushes in summer time that will cleave to a mans garments and creep into his Breeches eating themselves in a short time into the very flesh of a man.[11]

Even 30 years after the first explorations, visitors were still discovering wonders—abundant water, for example, and much safer to drink than in England. William Wood noted that the country was as "well watered as any land under the sun, every family or every two families having a spring of sweet waters betwixt them . . ." The water he thought of a "fatter substance and of a more jetty color [than in England]. Yet I dare not prefer it before good beer. . . . Those that drink it be as healthful, fresh and lusty as they that drink beer. These springs be not only within land but likewise bordering upon the seacoasts. . ."[12]

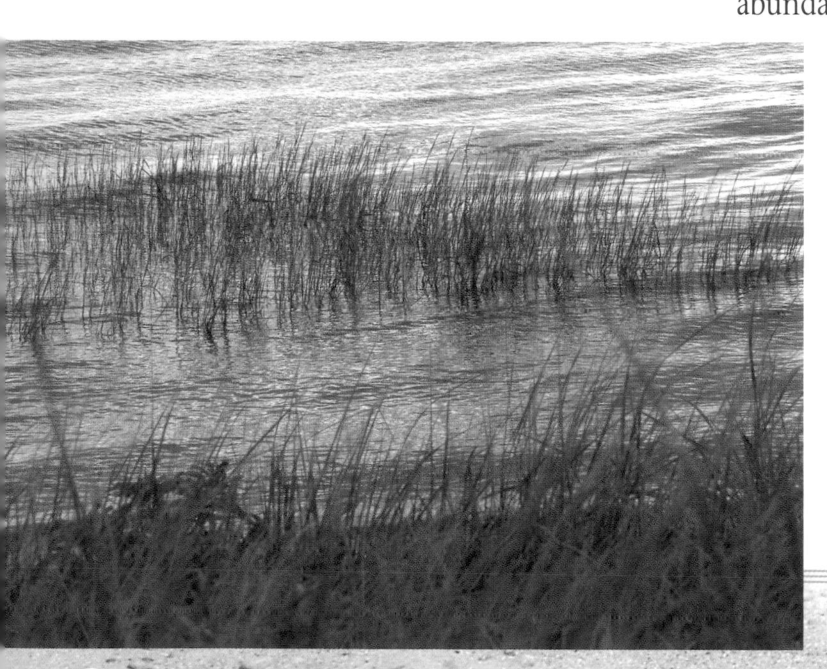

As late as the 1900s, the summer cottages on Duxbury Beach were advertised with their own water, and today Saquish property owners tap into fresh water only a few feet down.

Our area had other natural products that brought "good money." Pilgrim Edward Winslow, whose father was a successful English salt merchant, realized what "Salt House Beach" (the first, though short-lived, name for Duxbury Beach) offered. In pre-refrigeration days, salt was the only food preservative. Cod salted by the sailors would easily last the Atlantic home voyage and fetch good prices on European markets.

Champlain's map shows stands of thick timber on Gurnet Point—"Principally pine," he noted. Here was another of nature's give-a-ways, one of immediate domestic value. Back in England, only the wealthy few had light and crackling warm fires in winter. Here, pitch pine, also known as "candlewood," provided "splinter lights"—"very useful in a House," wrote one newcomer.

Pine had other uses as well. The tallest trees were cut for ships' masts. Turpentine was a common remedy for cuts and small wounds. Soon, however, the colonists realized that pines were necessary to stabilize beach sands, and by 1702, cutting pine on the beaches was strictly forbidden.

Even more valuable than pine was the local white oak. Many of the first homeward-bound ships were laden with oak barrel staves. These would be used everywhere for the storage and shipment of food and wine. Someone made the happy discovery that this wood, being quite porous, notably improved the taste of wine. After that, business flourished.

Once again, overcutting caused trouble. Justin Winsor, growing up in Duxbury, witnessed the decline of shipbuilding in the mid-1800s. He believed the depletion of local oak was a major contributing factor.

Last but not least of the area's natural wonders was grassland. However, after the arrival of cattle in 1627 (and a surprising assortment, including a red "cowe" and a "blind Heyter"), grazing land—especially on the beach—was at a premium. Overgrazing left the barrier beach, and thus the town, at risk. Justin Winsor reported that by the mid-1700s "several times the seed had been sown at different points, and even as early as 1751, the town took measures to prevent the grass being eaten by cattle. At a town meeting this year on the 20th of May they voted 'to petition the General Court to get an act to prevent neat cattle going upon or feeding on Duxbury Beach for the future . . .'"[13]

Thoreau on Seaweed

[The] kelp, oarweed, tangle, devil's-apron, sole-leather, or ribbon-weed—as various species are called—appeared to us a singularly marine and fabulous product. . . . [One] species looked almost edible; at least I thought that if I were starving I would try it. One sailor told me that the cows ate it. . . . I took the earliest opportunity to sit down and deliberately whittle up a fathom or two of it . . . [to see] if it were hollow all the way through. The blade looked like a broad belt . . . and it was also twisted spirally. . . . A piece of the stem which I carried home shrunk to one-quarter of its size a week afterward, and was completely covered with crystals of salt-like frost.

From ***Cape Cod***, by Henry David Thoreau,
"Observations from Walking Trips in 1849, 1850, 1855"
(New York; Thomas Crowell Co., 1966), pp. 78-79.

Timeline

1675 1686 1687

1675 – King Philip's War begins. Clark's Island is used as holding place for the praying Indians.

1686 – Plymouth Colony becomes part of the short-lived Dominion of New England.

1687 – Death of John Alden.

Endurance

Duxbury's barrier beach is a hard, hostile place. Yet here, despite battering seas and trampling wind, life not only endures but flourishes. Area plants find their basic requirements—food, water, shelter. Survival, if chancy, is always possible.

Nearest the wrack-spattered front line, dune grasses spike up through sand, nourished by the winter's accumulation of decayed seaweeds. Northeasters may destroy the young community, but beach heather—"poverty grass"—can hang on by the skin of its teeth.

Farther up the sloping dune, other plants have their life-sustaining strategies. The succulent beach pea has waxen leaves that can curl up for protection, "playing possum." Dusty miller, possibly a refugee from sedate gardens, is the quintessential beach lay-about sunning on its wooly mat.

By contrast to the exposed front dune, High Pines, probably named before 1637, seems almost a Garden of Eden. Wind-scooped hollows collect nutrients and moisture. Pitch pine and cedar provide a rough and ready shelter for thickets of beach rose, beach plum, that gleaming villain poison ivy, and bayberry, a shrub with roots rich in nitrogen.

The beach upland is at its brilliant best in autumn. Seaside goldenrod, watered through the dry weeks by underground seeps, offers rest and food for migrating monarch butterflies. Pockets of sky blue asters (a true "Native American" plant) may outwit frost and last into December.

In the bayside marshland, late summer flood tides float the spartinas' tall leaves. At low water, salt-tolerant salicornias turn smoldering coral while seaside lavender and seaside gerardia keep a weather watch.

What is the significance of this four-hundred-year record? Are beach and bay changed beyond all recognition?

Remarkably, much appears as it did to the first wayfarers. True, the Gurnet trees pictured by Champlain are gone, but High Pines maintains the same sturdy profile. A small white Arctic owl, first recorded in the 1600s, still hunts in the winter dunes (maybe the same owl? Methuselah!). Near the creek, the "sleeky" crane fishes patiently, and "sanderlins" scurry along the wrack line, no longer likely to become suet pudding. The piping plovers, with devoted human help, nest in the cobble—at the razor's edge of extinction every year. Insect "pesterments"—flies, "gurnippers," and "tikes"—continue to feed on us. In the bright gold dunes of September, monarch butterflies rest and feast before their incredible migratory journey.

The Sounds of Surf

Upon the south side of the sandy beach the sea beateth, which is a true prognostication to presage storms and foul weather and the breaking up of the frost. For when a storm hath been, or is likely to be, it will roar like thunder, being heard six miles; and after storms [the sea] casts up great store of great clams which the Indians, taking out of their shells, carry out in baskets.

William Wood, ***New England's Prospect*** (1634),
Ed. Alden T. Vaughn (Amherst, Mass.: University of Massachusetts Press, 1977), p. 62.

All morning we had heard the sea roar on the eastern shore, which was several miles distant; for it still felt the effects of the storm . . . , though a school-boy, whom we overtook, hardly knew what we meant, his ears were so used to it. He would have more plainly heard the same sound in a shell. It was a very inspiring sound to walk by, filling the whole air . . . instead of having a dog to growl before your door, to have an Atlantic Ocean. . . .

From ***Cape Cod***, by Henry David Thoreau,
"Observations from Walking Trips in 1849, 1850, 1855"
(New York; Thomas Crowell Co., 1966), pp. 78-79.

As the days shorten and the constellation Orion stalks the night sky, beach plant life lives on borrowed time. Awake or asleep, we are haunted by the boom of surf, for we know all too well the great waves that threaten the beach with destruction. But time and time again, committed rescuers have undertaken the back-breaking work of restoration—saving the kingdom by the sea.

Explorers of the beach are still wonderstruck by their discoveries in marine biology classes, Audubon field trips, and family walks. Children, too, are making their own discoveries on Duxbury Beach. They will follow a snail track, making the connection between land and sea. They will cherish an ancient yellow-striped "lucky stone."

The future depends on our experiences and what we learn from them. What matters most, however, is holding fast to the sense of wonder. Tomorrow is in good hands.

Timeline

1690

1694

1690 – Plymouth Colony becomes part of the Massachusetts Bay Colony.

1690 – Plymouth sells Clark's Island to Samuel Lucas, Elkanah Watson, and George Morton; Plymouth sells Saquish to Ephraim and George Morton.

1694 – Plymouth sells the Gurnet to John Doty, John Nelson, and Samuel Lucas.

Gallery

*Left and Below: Sea lavender (*Limonium carolinianum*). Tidal extremes do not disturb this native salt meadow plant.*

*Lower left: Beach plum (*Prunus maritima*). In early spring, white flower clusters show up before the leaves. Late summer fruit picked at just the right time and cooked by a skilled hand makes the region's famous jelly most delectable.*

*Left: Common mullein (*Verbascum thapsus*). Tall yellow flowers tower over gray flannel leaves.*

*Below left: American beach grass (*Ammophilia breviligulata*). Tagged a "lover of sand," beach grass is the staying force of the beach. To one observer, its autumn coloring resembles a fierce lion's ruff.*

*Below right: Red cedar (*Juniperus virgininiana*). This slow-growing tree is often wind-sculpted into strange shapes.*

Gallery

Beach roses (Rosa rugosa). This fragrant erosion control plant (also referred to as "salt spray roses") has red "hips" (above). It florishes in many areas along the back road to the Gurnet and Saquish.

Right and below left: Goldenrod (Solidago sempervirens): a late-season feeding station for migrating monarch butterflies.

Below right: Poison ivy (Rhus radicans) is perhaps the hardiest and most common plant on Duxbury Beach and Saquish. Contact with any part of this plant in any season may cause skin rashes or blisters.

3 Duxbury Beach... Dreamers & Schemers
The Early Years

During its long history, Duxbury Beach has attracted people of all kinds—from farmers of the 1600s and 1700s to modern-day windsurfers, and in between, in the late 1800s, a few dreamers and schemers who thought they knew how the beach could be "improved." Had these well-intentioned gentlemen had their way, Duxbury Beach would today be lined with cottages all the way to the Plymouth line. That they did not prevail is owing in large part to acts of nature and a few national financial crises.

Between 1637, when Duxbury was incorporated as a town, and 1919, when the Duxbury Beach Association was formed, the ownership of the beach changed at least half a dozen times. One of the earliest allusions to the value of this sandy strip dates from 1639, when the Plymouth Colony court ordered that the Gurnet, Saquish and Clark's Island "shall . . . remain unto the town of Plymouth." This was a warning to the people of Duxbury not to expect these areas to become part of their new

The view from the back road at High Pines is much the same today as in horse and buggy days. The Myles Standish Monument can be seen in the background of both photos.

Timeline

1712 1714 1715

1712 – Six Duxbury men drown off Duxbury Beach when their whaling boat capsizes.

November 20, 1714 – The common lands of Duxbury Beach are divided into 17 lots of 10 shares each.

1714 - 1715 – Many of the shareowners of Duxbury Beach convey their interest to Nathaniel Thomas of Kingston.

domain. Evidently, the residents of Plymouth did not want to share with residents of other towns the fish, game, timber, and salt hay that these areas afforded. Later in the century, however, Duxbury men did gain rights to some of the Gurnet's salt hay meadows.

By 1678, the eastern boundaries of Duxbury had been established, and as a result, the northern end of the outer beach became part of Marshfield. So, by the end of the 1600s, the beach—although known as Duxbury Beach—was jointly owned by Marshfield, Duxbury, and Plymouth. The beach in each town was common land, where residents went to fish, hunt, and gather salt hay for their cattle. The residents of Duxbury usually visited the outer beach by boat because the only other way, until the Powder Point Bridge was built in 1892, was the long way through Green Harbor in Marshfield.

In the early 1700s, Duxbury began to divide its common land, including parts of the outer beach and marsh areas, giving the rights to these properties to various Duxbury residents. After so many years of common ownership, one has to wonder what prompted this change. It seems to have been a combination of factors. When the town of Pembroke split from Duxbury in 1712, Duxbury's population dwindled, as did support for the minister and church, and at the same time, funds were needed to build a new meetinghouse. To increase its population and taxable property, to muster support for the church, and hopefully to keep the next generation in the vicinity, the town gave away its common land.

In 1714, Duxbury divided its part of the beach into 17 lots of 10 shares each, which were then given out by lottery to 130 Duxbury residents.[1] Most of the new owners soon sold their shares to Nathaniel Thomas of Kingston. From 1714 to 1832, several generations of the Thomas family were the private owners of Duxbury Beach. However, "the privilege of a [right of] way" existed down the beach from one end to the other, and residents of Duxbury and the neighboring towns continued to fish, hunt, and gather salt hay on the beach as if it were public property.

The Halfway House on Duxbury Beach

Halfway houses, originally called "huts of refuge," were small, simple shacks stocked with a few necessities such as food and firewood. The Massachusetts Humane Society built 17 of these huts from 1786 to 1807 along isolated stretches of the coast where shipwrecked mariners could seek shelter. Reports of a shipwrecked coastal sloop off Duxbury Beach in 1786 mention a small hut as being the reason nine men survived.

There is no further mention of huts until the Gurnet Life-Saving Station was established at Gurnet Point in 1878. A small shack located half a mile south of the present Powder Point Bridge was known as a "halfway house" because it marked the mid-point for patrols. Lifeguards from the station would walk to the hut, punch a small portable clock to show they had been there, and then return to the Gurnet.

In 1891, the Brant Rock Life-Saving Station was built. Four times a night, men from the two stations met at the halfway house and exchanged tokens as proof that they had completed their patrol. The Gurnet lifeguards often handed over letters to be posted at the Brant Rock Post Office. Years later, a telephone was installed at the halfway house since the telephone wires did not extend to Gurnet Point.

The halfway house on Duxbury Beach was several times destroyed by storms and rebuilt, lasting until the Gurnet Coast Guard Station ended its beach patrols in 1955. This snug halfway house, as small and insubstantial as it was, must have provided an oasis of warmth and comfort for those mariners and lifeguards who had to brave the dangerous seas and lonely stretches of Duxbury Beach.

Timeline

c. 1720 · 1738 · 1742

c. 1720 – The Burgess family builds the first house (the farmhouse) on the Gurnet.

1738 – Nathaniel Thomas conveys 88 shares of Duxbury Beach to his son, Nathaniel Thomas, Jr.

1742 – Benjamin Hanks buys the old farmhouse on Saquish and lives there for four years before moving out West.

The Cut River Canal

Who today would suspect that some of the waterways near the Duxbury-Marshfield line are man-made? The name "Cut River" provides a clue to its origin, and the Cut River Canal (mentioned in documents from 1636) is the first canal dug in this country.

The Cut River, one of the small, tidal creeks extending deep into the Duxbury marsh, lies just west of the northernmost end of Duxbury Beach. Early colonists were quick to recognize that the short distance between a bend of this river and the Green Harbor River offered the possibility of an inland waterway between Plymouth Harbor and the coastal towns to the north. Widening of the serpentine creek began in 1632. The Plymouth Colony Laws for 1636 record that "It is also ordered by the Court that the Cut at Green Harbor for a boat passage shall be made eighteen feet wide and six foot deep."

The new canal did away with the need to venture around Gurnet Point, into the dangerous open waters off Duxbury Beach. By sailing north through Duxbury Bay, into the Pine Point River and then the Cut River, colonists from Plymouth could reach the Green Harbor River and travel upstream to inland settlements in Marshfield. It was even possible to go from there to Scituate via the South River.

By 1850, larger ships and the rebuilt twin lighthouses on Gurnet Point had made the inland route obsolete, but you may still see the Cut River Canal from the small bridge near the end of Canal Street in Marshfield, just before the road passes into Duxbury and becomes Gurnet Road.

In 1832, several of Nathaniel Thomas's great-grandchildren sold to the town of Duxbury for $150 their right and title to "any and every part of Duxbury Beach, so called, which lays within the limits of said town." Although boundaries are unclear in this and earlier deeds, it is clear that this portion of the beach was Duxbury's share from the Marshfield town line to the Plymouth town line.

At a time when Duxbury's reputation as a shipbuilding center was at its peak, the outer beach once again became a town-owned public place. Most residents continued to go there by boat because the ride through Marshfield over the Cut River Canal bridge was long and difficult. But as the 1800s progressed, more and more Duxbury townspeople took the long route for the pleasure of the carriage ride, the invigorating fresh air, and the stunning beauty of the remote beach.

For almost 40 years, the town of Duxbury remained the sole owner of most of the beach. During that time, the town went from being a thriving shipbuilding center to a quiet backwater. A major reason for the decline in this mainstay of the economy was that the waters of Duxbury Bay were not deep enough to accommodate the larger and faster clipper ships that shipyards in Boston and other deep-water ports were producing.

The post-Civil War years—the era of Reconstruction—brought a resurgence of energy to Duxbury. While the nation's attention was focused on railroad building and fortunes were being made or lost through investments in commerce, the idea took hold in Duxbury that the beach needed to be developed and "improved." Foremost among the promoters of this idea was Stephen Gifford. Gifford believed that the way to blow the dust off the town and revive its economy was to take advantage of its biggest natural resource—the beach. As clerk of the Massachusetts Senate, Gifford was an influential man, and it was through his connections that the agents of the French Cable Company chose Duxbury Beach as the French Atlantic Cable's final destination.

By the end of the 1860s, commerce and big business had literally come ashore at Duxbury Beach. Pauline Winsor Wilkinson, who grew up in Duxbury wrote, "After the French cable landed on Duxbury Beach there was a great celebration, and we thought it would build up the town."[2] And so it did, at least in the short term.

For the next three years, from 1869 to 1872, Duxbury was in a real estate frenzy. At the town meeting in March 1871, the townspeople, hoping to capitalize on the real estate boom, voted to sell a portion of Duxbury Beach—15 acres up against the Marshfield line known for many years as Cut Island and since 1872 as Webster Island—to developers who wanted to divide it into lots for summer cottages. The developers, Bryant and Dwinnell, were already building up Green Harbor and Brant Rock with cottages in anticipation of the arrival of the Duxbury and Cohasset Railroad. The railroad was

Timeline

1743 — 1751 — 1768

1743 – Nathaniel Thomas, Jr. dies, leaving "Gurnet meadow and beach adjoining" to his widow and two children, John and Hannah.

May 20, 1751 – Town of Duxbury passes law that prohibits cattle from grazing on Duxbury Beach.

1768 – Construction begins on the first lighthouse at the Gurnet, on land belonging to the Thomas family.

The French Atlantic Cable Comes to Duxbury

In 1868, the French-owned Ocean Telegraph Company was seeking a landing point somewhere between Boston and Provincetown for the first transatlantic cable from Europe to the United States. An agent of the company met with Plymouth historian William T. Davis for advice on possible landing sites. Davis, according to his own account, immediately suggested Duxbury Beach—still known at the time as Salt House Beach—as an ideal location. He arranged for a local fisherman who was well-acquainted with the beach to meet with a director of the French company. The director was pleased with the geography and immediately decided to buy a parcel of land at the north end of the beach, at a place locals called "Rouse's Hummock." The location was kept secret so as not to fan speculation.

Duxbury residents Gershom Weston, son of Ezra Weston II, and Stephen Gifford, clerk of the Massachusetts Senate, were let in on the plans and acted as go-betweens for the cable company and selectmen. At first, the selectmen were suspicious of the project and refused to sell. However, once they were given details of the cable crossing, they changed their minds and convinced town meeting to sell the beach parcel to Gifford and his business associate, William Dexter of Brookline. Gifford and Dexter transferred the parcel to the Ocean Telegraph Company just 11 days before the cable came ashore.

The French Atlantic Cable arrived on July 23, 1869, to great fanfare. It was hauled onto the beach and across a ridge to Rouse's Hummock, where a small hut had been built to hold the motors and mechanical equipment. From that time on, Rouse's Hummock has been known as Cable Hill.

The cable was then laid across the creeks and marshes of the Back River, and on July 27, muddy work crews dragged the cable up Abrams Hill, where a crowd of 600 dignitaries,

The French Atlantic Cable arrives on Duxbury Beach on July 23, 1869.

including the governor and mayor of Boston, were cheering its arrival. The festivities continued that evening at a ball held at the Wright estate on St. George Street.

A few days after the celebration, the cable was brought down the hill and into the Old Cove Street town landing. From there it was laid down Cove Street to the old Weston Bank Building at the corner of Washington and St. George Streets. This building, which housed the operators, has been known since then as the Cable House.

The Duxbury terminal of the French Atlantic Cable brought some measure of fame to the town, but not the commercial development some had predicted. It served faithfully through the end of World War II, transmitting telegraph messages between the continents, even when faster and more efficient means of communication were emerging. If it were not for the perfect location of Duxbury Beach, the colorful era of the French Atlantic Cable might never have become part of Duxbury's history.

rushed to completion in August 1871, just in time for the groundbreaking of the Myles Standish Monument, high on Captain's Hill. It was reported that 10,000 people trooped up to the summit for the ceremony. The culminating event of that very eventful year was a special town meeting held in September at which the townspeople voted to sell all 200 acres of Duxbury Beach to Boston businessman Stephen Allen.

Stephen Allen was a poster boy for his generation of entrepreneurial businessmen. He grew up poor in New Hampshire, earned a law degree, and ended up making a fortune in Boston real estate. He married well and dabbled in ideas for a synthetic cotton material. Allen most likely came to Duxbury because of his friendships with the Gifford and Wright families. Once here, he quickly bought up land, driving up land prices, and assembled an imposing summer estate on the old Myles Standish

Timeline

1773 — 1775-1783

1773 – John Thomas of Plymouth, son of Nathaniel, conveys to his sister Hannah's husband, John Thomas of Kingston, 39 acres of the Gurnet, including the land on which the lighthouse stands.

1775-1783 – American Revolution. Duxbury and surrounding towns mostly support the revolutionaries.

At right is a photo taken in the aftermath of the Boston Fire of 1872. Stephen Allen suffered heavy losses and had to abandon his dream of developing cottage lots on Duxbury Beach.

At far right is a plan drawn in 1888 showing cottage lots proposed for Duxbury Beach.

Stephen Gifford and John Loring, a wealthy lumber merchant who lived along the Bluefish River. We can only guess what their master plan for the beach was, but 20 years before a bridge was actually built across Duxbury Bay, they evidently were dreaming about it as a way of opening up the beach to development.

farm. He was the key figure in seeing that great fanfare and publicity attended the ground-breaking ceremony for the Myles Standish Monument.

Shrewd businessman that he was, Allen was able to convince the town that by developing cottage lots, private enterprise could "improve" the beach and thereby benefit the town. The town subsequently sold him the beach for $3,100, which included a $2,500 mortgage. Allen then quickly resold it, in early 1872, to what was known as the "Duxbury Beach and Bridge Company." Trustees of that company were Duxbury's own

Whatever dreams Gifford, Loring, and Allen might have had for Duxbury Beach went up in smoke with two events: the Boston Fire of 1872 and the Financial Panic of 1873, which engulfed the entire country. Stephen Allen was among those who lost heavily in the Boston fire; for years afterward, the town of Duxbury chased him for unpaid real estate taxes. The rush on banks that occurred in 1873 put another coffin nail in plans for "improving" Duxbury Beach. Even at the northern end of the beach, very few lots were sold. At the end of the 1870s, most of Duxbury Beach remained a wild landscape, almost untamed by human beings.

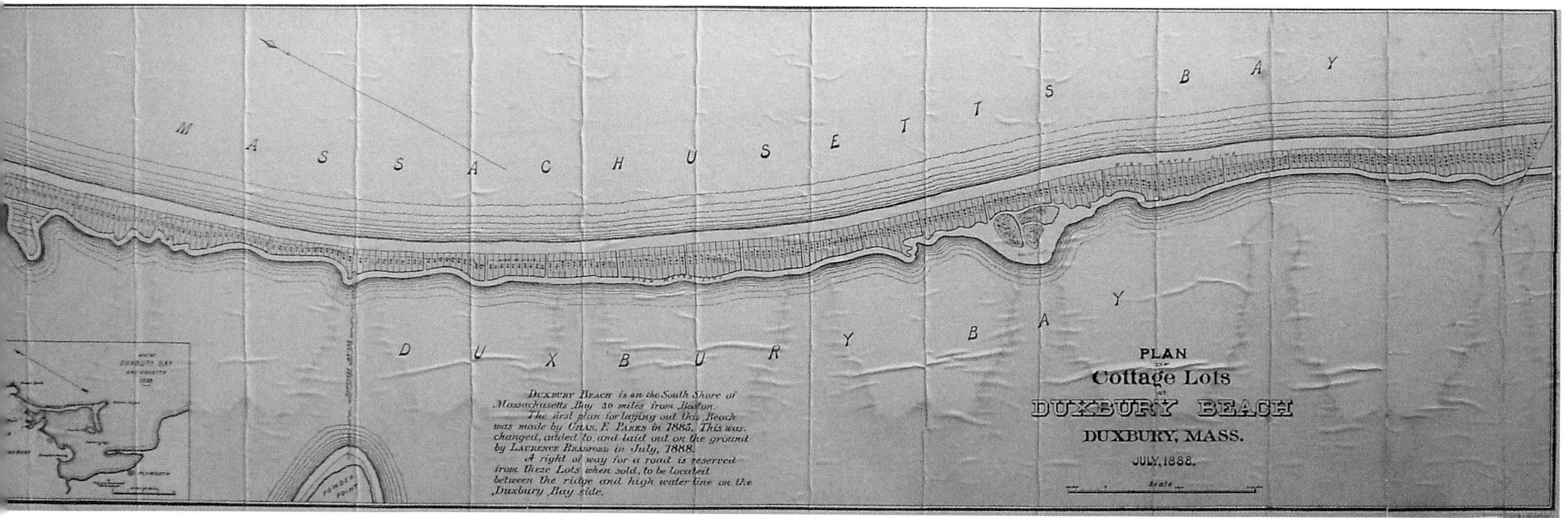

The 1880s were a slow time for Duxbury. Like the rest of the country, the town suffered the repercussions of another major financial crisis in 1884. A further setback to the grand plans for Duxbury Beach occurred in April 1886, when Stephen Gifford died unexpectedly of pneumonia. Duxbury did finally vote in 1887 to build a road (now known as Gurnet Road) from the Marshfield town line to Cable Hill (the new name for Rouse's Hummock after the arrival of the French Atlantic Cable) in hopes of stirring interest in development—but to little avail.

George Wright, an influential Duxbury resident who had inherited money and who made a fortune on his own in cotton brokering before and after the Civil War, took over the mortgage on Duxbury Beach in 1887. Soon after that, the Wright family built three substantial summer cottages in the vicinity of High Pines. These were to be the "model" cottages for further beach development, but they were unlived in most of the time. The Wright family visited their cottages only occasionally—on some very hot summer days or when they might host a beach picnic.

William Wright, George's nephew, was the family member who pursued the "improvement" of Duxbury Beach with relentless energy and seemingly boundless funds. At the town meeting of 1889, the people of Duxbury passed a resolution stating that they "regard with

1776 – John Thomas of Kingston, Major General and Commander in Chief of the American Army in Canada, dies, leaving his widow Hannah to care for the lighthouse.

1776 – The towns of Duxbury, Kingston, and Plymouth build Fort Andrew, a six-cannon battery on the Gurnet.

August 7, 1782 – 24-year-old Horatio Nelson, captain of the *Albemarle*, captures but later releases Master Nathaniel Carver's Plymouth schooner *Harmony* off the Gurnet.

Timeline

1776

1782

Beach Houses Floated Across Bay

When the Duxbury Beach Association took ownership of the beach from the Wright estate in 1919, the purchase included three houses the Wright family had built near High Pines in the late 1880s. These houses were the models for 263 cottages the Wrights planned to build on the beach after the Powder Point Bridge was constructed. Although the Wrights never built these cottages, they did occasionally use the three model homes to entertain their summer guests.

At first, the Association leased the three houses, but what little rent it collected was not enough to cover maintenance, taxes, and insurance. On top of that, the houses were broken into from time to time. No longer wanting to be landlords, the Association voted on January 20, 1926, to sell all three houses to Duxbury resident Walter G. Prince for $1,500, provided he remove them before June 1. In a legendary feat, Prince floated the three houses on barges across Duxbury Bay and around Standish Shore to a lane off Bay Road, known henceforth as Landing Road. The houses still stand there today.

The Powder Point correspondent for the Old Colony Memorial *newspaper wrote these nostalgic words about the relocation of the three houses:*

> The old familiar sky-line along the Outer Beach has greatly changed since the departure of the famous "two houses" and the house at High Pines. These were landmarks. Although they had been vacant for some time and did not serve a very practical purpose in so isolated a place, we wonder how we can get along without them. Where shall we fly now when, way down the beach, we are overtaken by a thunder-shower, lacking the hospitable piazzas of the "two houses"? Also, and this is most serious, how can we possibly decide how far down the beach to walk when we haven't the houses to go by? And how can we sail up the channel at half-tide and not go aground, without the house to line up for our course? And then too, how will the future generation know what we are talking about when we charge them not to walk "any farther than the two houses"?

The Powder Point correspondent,
Old Colony Memorial, June 11, 1926.

At left are the Wright cottages on the beach, and above as they appear today on Landing Road.

satisfaction the efforts of Mr. William Wright to utilize Duxbury Beach by offering for sale building lots and erecting private houses there."[3] In 1892, after a long struggle with the Plymouth County Commissioners and after personally funding one-third of the cost of construction, William Wright was finally able to fulfill his long-held dream of a bridge connecting Duxbury to Duxbury Beach.

Although "improvement" of Duxbury Beach now seemed inevitable, hard economic times again acted as a deterrent. The final and perhaps most punishing blow to visions of cottages lining the beach all the way to the Plymouth line was the work of nature: the great Portland Gale of 1898.

Over the next 20 years, the Wright family dwindled. George Wright died in 1897 at age 72. William Wright married George's widow Georgianna in 1900. He died in 1912. All the Wright children were dead by 1916. Georgianna Wright

1786 – Death of Hitty Tom, the last Native American in the Duxbury area.

1790 – Newly formed U.S. government takes control of Gurnet Lighthouse.

March 11, 1792 – The *Columbia* is shipwrecked on High Pines Ledge; 2 sailors are saved, 14 drown.

Timeline 1786 1790 1792

was the last of the family and lived, alone and sick, much of the time at her residences in New York and Boston, where she died in 1919.

Although the Wrights rarely, if ever, came to Duxbury Beach during their last years of ownership, others did. Duck blinds and hunting camps cropped up along remote stretches of the beach, and cottage development started up again on the Webster Island lots. Squatters and fishermen built shacks and small cottages farther south, nearer the bridge; some had permission to do so, but some did not. Although the Wright family owned all 200 acres of Duxbury Beach, there were never any attempts, or at least any recorded attempts, to keep anyone off the beach.

By 1919, Duxbury Beach was still a relatively pristine, lonely stretch of sand, sea, and sky. Fishing, hunting, and salt-marsh haying continued as usual, as they had for hundreds of years. But because of the bridge, more and more people were visiting the beach, especially in the summer months, to enjoy ocean"bathing," carriage riding, and—by the turn of the twentieth century—automobile rides and roadster racing on the hard sand at low tide.

The year 1919 was a watershed year for the future of Duxbury Beach. In the aftermath of World War I, the idea that the beach could be improved by opening it up to development was replaced by a more complex concept: to keep the beach as close as possible to its natural state and yet allow people to use and enjoy it—a delicate balancing act that the Duxbury Beach Association and its successor, the Duxbury Beach Reservation, have been performing since 1919.

Duxbury Beach's real value for countless generations, whether publicly or privately owned, whether for wealthy schemers or footloose dreamers, has fed, "improved," and refreshed the souls of all who have laid eyes on its restless dunes and marshes and its endless stretches of sea and sky.

THE WRIGHT FAMILY

The Wright Estate on St. George Street, now the site of Duxbury High School.

The Wright family owned Duxbury Beach for over 30 years, beginning in 1887 when George Wright acquired the beach through foreclosure sales. Wright had grown up in Brookline and spent his active business life in the burgeoning commerce of New York City. Already wealthy from the family's dry goods trade, he and his brother made another fortune in cotton brokering during the boom years around the Civil War. He "retired" in 1868 and brought his family to live in Duxbury. They bought a former Weston family mansion on St. George Street and transformed it and the surrounding grounds into an opulent estate complete with marble fountains, greenhouses, and walnut-paneled stalls for their horses. Although they called Duxbury home, the Wright family also owned houses in Brookline, Boston's Back Bay, and New York City.

George Wright threw himself into the life of his adopted town by hosting a number of celebrations at his Pine Hill estate, including a sumptuous ball on July 23, 1869, the night the French Atlantic Cable was brought ashore. He was also part of a group of residents who wished to pump life and commerce into Duxbury by developing real estate. His plans were cut short when he died of pneumonia in 1897 at the age of 72.

William Wright, a nephew of George, and long a part of the Wright household, married George's widow Georgianna in 1900. William, like his uncle, took an active interest in Duxbury affairs. He developed cottage lots on Powder Point and was the force behind the building of the Powder Point Bridge. He was interested in horse racing and farming, and was known throughout Duxbury for his personal generosity. On a wider stage, he served as representative to the Massachusetts legislature. He was only 66 years old when he died of a heart attack in 1912.

The heart and soul of the family was Georgianna Wright. Her four children by George Wright were the center of her life, but sadly, three of the children died young in tragic circumstances. In response to personal tragedy, Georgianna Wright turned her energies to philanthropy. She built and endowed the handsome Wright building as a town library in 1909, endowed a chair at Princeton, and donated paintings to Boston's Museum of Fine Arts. Georgianna Wright's later years were clouded by illness and more sadness after her only remaining daughter died in 1916. She began to spend more time in New York and Boston, where she died in 1919 at the age of 82.

Timeline

1795 — 1801 — 1803

1795 – Benjamin Alden draws first local map of Duxbury, including Duxbury Beach.

1801 – Gurnet Lighthouse is destroyed by fire.

1803 – Gurnet Lighthouse is rebuilt.

Literary Duxbury Beach

The natural beauty of Duxbury Beach has inspired well-known writers over the years to express themselves in various literary forms. One of the first was Justin Winsor, *who in his 1849 book* History of Duxbury *gathered knowledge about the beach and town from many different sources, including older residents who remembered key information from far back into the eighteenth century.*

Henry David Thoreau *made numerous visits to the Watson family on Clark's Island in the early 1850s, and during these visits he frequently walked on Duxbury Beach. There he learned about horseshoe crabs, clamming, lobster houses (traps), and lobstering. He also heard piping plovers, gathered Irish moss, explored the old Revolutionary fort ruins on the Gurnet, and watched horses being swum across the channel to Clark's Island. He learned the joys of sailing and came to understand the meaning of "waiting for the tide," as all activities were governed by the time of high or low tide. Thoreau also understood the phrase "rut of the sea," as he listened to the powerful roar of the surf break onto the beach's sandy shore. The time Thoreau spent on Duxbury Beach clearly influenced his writing about seashore life in his book* Cape Cod, *published in 1864.*

Paul Brodeur, *a well-known nature writer for the* New Yorker, *wrote a touching remembrance of Duxbury Beach in 1959.* "A War Story" *tells of his family's spending the summer of 1942 at a cottage on the Gurnet Road end of Duxbury Beach. Brodeur wrote of the natural joys of the beach for him and his younger brother, but he also tells a harrowing story of their being caught in an old duck hunting camp beyond High Pines during a major army target bombardment practice on the beach. When the two small boys emerged from the hidden camp, they brought the practice to a shocked halt. Their rescue and subsequent canny blackmail of the commanding brigadier general in order to hang out with the army troops, resulted in a summer-long friendship with the chagrined troops, who made the boys' summer of '42 glow.*

In the 1950s, several columnists wrote regularly about Duxbury Beach. Willard DeLue *of the* Boston Globe *and* Henry Craig Walker *of the* Duxbury Clipper *wrote evocatively about many different aspects of the beach, such as what Duxbury Beach is like in winter, sleeping on the beach on a summer's night, or being on the beach during a fierce nor'easter storm. These mood pieces caught the many changeable faces of Duxbury Beach.*

The renowned poet Elizabeth Bishop *took a long walk on Duxbury Beach on a bitter March day in 1975 and was inspired to create a highly praised poem called* "The End of March," *which describes Duxbury Beach on a raw spring day when few would venture into the cutting wind.*

Duxbury children's author and illustrator Brian Lies *also evokes Duxbury Beach in his 2006* New York Times *best-seller picture book,* Bats at the Beach. *The bats come out to play at night on a beach very similar to Duxbury Beach, fondly bringing to mind similar human adventures for audiences of all ages.*

From bats to bitter winds, Duxbury Beach has spurred writers to heights of creativity with its wonders of the seashore world.

Gallery

Friends relax on the rocks at the base of the Gurnet, c. 1890.

A lumber schooner docked at Duxbury Coal & Lumber Co. wharf, c. 1910. Ships such as these would have been a common sight off Duxbury Beach in the 1800s.

Gallery

Looking north from the Gurnet, c. 1930. The house in the center left is the "old farmhouse."

Enjoying a day at the beach in the early 1900s.

Sailing in Duxbury Bay at the turn of the twentieth century.

Stereopticon slides were very popular in the mid- to late-nineteenth century. These slides (along with the slide shown on page 29) show the landing of the French Atlantic Cable at Rouse's Hummock in 1869. A stereopticon viewer is shown below.

Below: The coiled cable, ready to be carried across the Back River marsh to the Cable House on Washington Street.

Gallery

Right: A regatta on Duxbury Bay in 1899.

Below: The Duxbury Coal & Lumber Co. yard and the Duxbury Yacht Club, with participants of the Mid-Summer Series race, August, 1929.

Eben Ellison, Harriet Ellison, and Priscilla Soule playing on the beach in July 1900. (Girl at left is unidentified.)

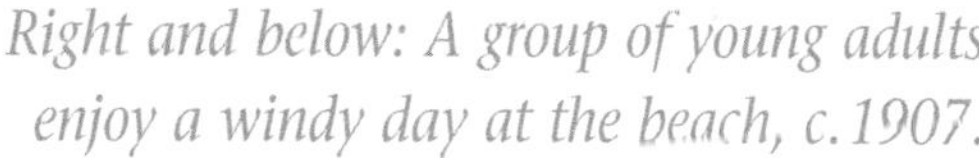

Right and below: A group of young adults enjoy a windy day at the beach, c.1907.

Gallery

DUXBURY BEACH.

FOR SALE OR TO LET, ON DUXBURY BEACH—Three new houses, finished in hard wood, amply furnished, and good water supply. For particulars apply to BLAKE & BRADFORD, 19 Exchange place, Boston; or Mr. WILLIAM J. WRIGHT, Duxbury, Mass. my 10 [u]FSTuThS

Duxbury Beach.

FOR SALE OR TO LET on Duxbury Beach Three new houses, finished in hardwood, amply furnished, and good water supply. For particulars apply to BLAKE & BRADFORD, 19 Exchange Place, Boston, or MR. WILLIAM J. WRIGHT, Duxbury, Mass. 19v2*

Two of the three Wright cottages on Duxbury Beach, c. 1885. The High Pines cottage is under construction in the top left photo. The photo in the lower left shows the house finished, and in the background are the two other cottages, one of which is also pictured in the upper-right photo. The two advertisements above appeared in local papers at the turn of the twentieth century.

Mapping Duxbury Beach: the 1780 DesBarres map, left; the 1833 Ford map, center; and the 1903 Plymouth County Atlas map, right.

4

DUXBURY BEACH...

The Bridge Across the Bay

History of the Powder Point Bridge

The Powder Point Bridge has always been a treasured Duxbury landmark, so much so that in 1987 residents voted unanimously to reconstruct it, replicating the original design and wooden construction.

The original bridge—in the beginning called "Gurnet Bridge" and sometimes "Long Bridge" or the "Half-Mile Bridge" —was built in 1892 by the Gurnet Bridge Company, which was incorporated in 1887 by an act and resolve of the Massachusetts legislature. The town of Duxbury, Plymouth County, and Duxbury resident William Wright each paid one-third of the project, which cost $30,000.

Wright had plans to build 263 houses on Duxbury Beach, which his uncle George Wright had purchased in 1887. A bridge across Duxbury Bay would shorten the 8-mile route through Marshfield to just under half a mile. At a special town meeting on April 20, 1888, Duxbury voters passed a resolution 65 to 46 in support of Wright's plan to construct a bridge. Whereas plans for the bridge were carried out, the Portland Gale in 1898 and a brutal northeaster the following winter caused Wright to cancel his plans for building the cottages.

The new Powder Point Bridge in 2006 and the original bridge (inset), c. 1915.

Timeline

1807-1808

1819

1807-1808 – Embargo Act closes American ports, causing an economic slowdown in shipbuilding towns like Duxbury.

1819 – Mrs. Hannah Thomas dies, and the property on Gurnet and Duxbury Beach is divided among her children, John, Nathaniel, and Hannah (Mrs. Zepheniah Willis).

Pilings for Duxbury Bridge

From Herman Delano's Diary . . .

Oct. 6, 1891

Went into the woods and cut 6 piles on P. Alden lot at $1.50 apiece, total of $9. Drawn the piles to foot of hill and left them. Had lame back.

Oct. 7, 1891

The 2 boys, Herman and Leavitt, have gone down with teams and drawed in 6 piles from P. Alden lot at $4 each (total $24).

These pilings were the first two loads of pile that were used to build the Gurnet Bridge in 1892. There were a total of 125 piles at $4 each.

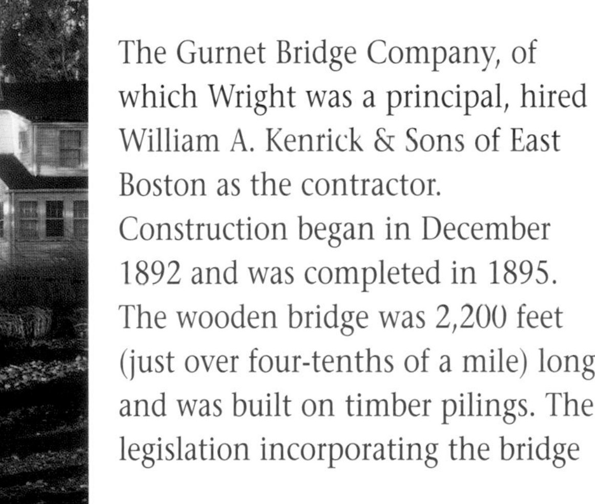

The Gurnet Bridge Company, of which Wright was a principal, hired William A. Kenrick & Sons of East Boston as the contractor. Construction began in December 1892 and was completed in 1895. The wooden bridge was 2,200 feet (just over four-tenths of a mile) long and was built on timber pilings. The legislation incorporating the bridge company called for the bridge to be at least 20 feet wide with a "suitable draw therein with a clear width of not less than 24 feet for the passage of vessels."[1] The "draw" was constructed over the channel and was manually operated. A sailor who wanted to get under the bridge would have to tie the boat to a piling, climb a ladder to the bridge deck, raise the draw, sail the boat to the other side, and then climb the bridge again

Left: The "draw," as it was called, after being washed into the bay during a winter storm in 1957.

to lower the draw. The draw fell into disrepair in the 1930s, serving only as a diving platform for youth until finally collapsing into the bay in 1957.

From the beginning, the bridge was a popular addition to the town, although townspeople did not care for the name "Gurnet Bridge" and soon took to calling it "Long Bridge" and eventually the "Powder Point Bridge." In the early days, horse-drawn vehicles carried beach goers, but then came the automobile. Visitors parked their Model T's on the bridge and along the roads leading to it until the Duxbury Beach Association constructed a parking lot at the east end of the bridge in 1931.

In 1904, the Massachusetts legislature transferred ownership of the bridge to Plymouth County. The act called for maintenance costs to be shared one-third by Plymouth County, one-third by the town of Duxbury, and one-third by the towns of Plymouth, Marshfield, and Kingston. Bridge maintenance did occur over the decades, with over 100 new piles added in 1917, 125 piles installed in 1928, and more than 200 piles placed in 1938. It was at that point that the Plymouth County Commissioners expressed concern over increasing repair costs. They acknowledged that Gurnet and Saquish residents (residents of

1832 – U.S. Senator Daniel Webster from Marshfield obtains federal funds for first dune restoration project on the beach—a wall of seaweed stacked between parallel rows of fencing.

July 25, 1832 - Town of Duxbury acquires Duxbury beach for $150 from John Thomas and his sister Hannah.

1843 – Gurnet Lighthouse is rebuilt as two octagonal towers, with a corridor between them.

Timeline

1832 1843

Plymouth) needed access to their homes, but they also noted with disapproval that the bridge provided access to a private beach. At a county conference in 1938, selectmen from Plymouth, Kingston, and Marshfield also expressed concern over the rising repair costs. They proposed that Duxbury take over all responsibility for the bridge. A short time later, Duxbury voters at annual town meeting agreed to take control of the bridge and assume the maintenance costs, and through another act of the Massachusetts legislature in 1941, ownership of the bridge was transferred to the town.

The town maintained the bridge for the next 30 years and in 1971 hired a consultant to survey the condition of the bridge. The report was not good: it recommended replacing 360 pilings and performing deck repairs at an estimated cost of $240,000. Voters at town meeting did not appropriate the money.

The bridge continued to deteriorate and repeated inspections revealed increasing structural problems. In 1975, a group of Duxbury residents formed the Build Your Own Bridge (BYOB) Committee and made several attempts to get needed repairs done. It was not until 1985, when a fire believed to have been started by a fisherman's lantern damaged 200 feet of the bridge, that the town made substantial repairs. However, when state inspectors examined the repaired sections, they found additional weaknesses in other sections of the bridge. The state officially closed the bridge on July 23, 1985.

At that grave moment in bridge history, remnants of the original BYOB Committee recruited other residents to take action. Several weeks later, on September 16, 1985, the Board of Selectmen held a special town meeting, and voters unanimously agreed to transfer $250,000 from the town's Reserve Overlay Fund to pay for an engineering study of the bridge. In October, a group from the reenergized BYOB Committee met with the Board of Selectmen and offered to form a

Ironing the Bridge

After a particularly ice-cluttered winter some years ago, we can all remember hillocks on the bridge where in one place you could not see a person approaching until you had come to the brow of a wooden hill. This presented a staggering problem when spring came and the bridge having been boosted clean out of the mud in places, hung uncertainly on this high section. . . . We were at the lunch table when the crescendo of racket brought us to the door and we saw the good old City of Brockton reeling slowly down through the dust. The steam roller literally ironed out the humps in the bridge. It pressed the bridge back into the mud and there it has remained ever since, though why the ice floes in March do not boost it off its legs every year, I cannot possibly fathom.

Old Colony Memorial, January 23, 1936.

reconstruction committee. The selectmen agreed and appointed the Powder Point Bridge Committee.

The new committee selected an engineering design firm that presented five alternatives for a replacement bridge. Two designs were for concrete bridges, two were for steel spans, and one was for a wooden bridge. The committee liked the wooden design because it replicated the beloved old bridge and featured tropical hardwoods that were resistant to marine borers and fire.

The committee presented the alternatives to town meeting in the spring of 1986 and received approval for the hardwood design and an appropriation of $3 million for building costs. Construction began in the late fall of 1986 but was fraught with problems, including disputes over the competitive bidding process and delays in receiving the imported hardwood. Nevertheless, the problems were overcome, and a newly constructed Powder Point Bridge was dedicated on August 29, 1987.

The bridge won several architectural awards for its design. The new bridge is 2,200 feet long, the same as the old one, but 2 feet higher to accommodate rising sea levels. There is a 5- to 6-foot rise over the channel to allow for passage of small sailboats. This slight incline also provides a view of the ocean when driving over the bridge, and it enhances the horizontal view of the bridge against the horizon. To protect walkers from vehicles, the sidewalk is a foot higher than the previous sidewalk. It is also a foot wider to accommodate wheelchairs. The railings have three rails instead of two

Timeline

1849 1861 1868

1849 – Justin Winsor's *A History of Duxbury* is published.

1861 – Civil War begins, and Fort Standish, a rectangular earthwork, is erected on Saquish Head.

1868 – Wright family arrives in Duxbury and buys a Weston family mansion on what is now St. George Street.

for added safety. Another interesting feature of the new bridge is that square pilings support it rather than the round pilings used in the original bridge.

Twenty years into its new life, the bridge has had no significant repairs. However, the Commonwealth of Massachusetts recently lowered its carrying load rating, and piling repair is scheduled to take place. Those who love the Powder Point Bridge and the original, historic Gurnet Bridge will need to be vigilant about keeping this magnificent structure regularly inspected and maintained. It is a treasure and an important part of the town's heritage.

The Longest Wooden Bridge in the World?

You do not have to stand long on Powder Point Bridge before hearing a passerby claim that it is the longest wooden bridge in the United States or North America or even the world. In the early twentieth century, there were at least two wooden bridges in the United States longer than Powder Point Bridge. A 2 ½ mile wooden bridge crossed Biscayne Bay in Miami, and a wooden bridge just short of a mile in length connected Hampton Beach in New Hampshire to neighboring beaches. These bridges, however, eventually were replaced with steel and cement structures. The Guinness Book of World Records *includes a record for the longest wooden footbridge, a 2,944-foot structure in Japan. But at 2,200 feet—same as the original bridge—the Powder Point Bridge indeed appears to be the longest wooden bridge in America, if not the world, open to vehicular traffic.*

Gallery

Right: The Powder Point Bridge, c. 1917. At that time cars were allowed to park on the bridge.

Below: A view of Powder Point, c. 1910, taken from the bridge looking southwest toward the Myles Standish Monument.

Gallery

The original bridge, completed in 1895, was first called Gurnet Bridge, then Long Bridge, and, finally, the Powder Point Bridge.

Demolition of the old bridge began in late fall of 1986. The decking and stringers were removed first, and the old piles were left as markers for the new bridge.

The bridge decking was preassembled in Fairhaven, Massachusetts, and brought to the bridge on huge flatbeds. Cranes lowered the deck sections or "bents" onto the stringers attached to the pilings.

Gallery

Tropical hardwoods were used to build the new bridge because of their resistance to fire and marine borers. The square pilings are Dicoiymia, known commercially as Basralocus. The piles of the old bridge were removed at the same time the new piles were driven in.

The deck and railings were constructed using Lophira alata, a hardwood known commercially as Bongossi.

5 Duxbury Beach... The Great Storms

Assaults on a Ribbon of Sand

Every 50 to 100 years on average, New England is struck by a storm that does catastrophic damage to the coastline. The extent of damage Duxbury Beach will sustain during one of these storms is related to such factors as height of the tide, the force and direction of the wind, wind speed in relation to high tide, and the duration of the storm. So, while a storm with heavy easterly winds (75 miles or higher) striking at low tide, as Hurricane Bob did in August 1991, will cause minimal damage, a storm with heavy winds out of the east or northeast during an above-normal high tide can cause considerable destruction. The waves that build up from continuous easterly winds are so powerful when they strike the shore that the tide cannot go out. When the next high tide comes in, it may be several feet above normal. This phenomenon occurred in the Portland Gale of 1898, the Blizzard of 1978, and the No-Name Storm of 1991. In the Blizzard of '78, the east winds blew for nearly four days. In the No-Name Storm, the east winds continued for five days.

"After the storm." The wind has shifted from the east and northeast to the northwest.

Timeline

1868

1869

1868 – The French-owned Ocean Telegraph Company chooses Duxbury Beach as the landing site for the French Atlantic Cable.

July 27, 1869 – The French Atlantic Cable comes ashore at Rouse's Hummock, thereafter called Cable Hill, and is carried across the marsh to Abrams Hill, where a huge celebration takes place.

Which Is Worse for the Beach... Nor'easters or Hurricanes?

The coast of Massachusetts is susceptible to two types of storms that have the potential to cause significant damage to barrier beaches. The most prevalent storm is the northeaster, which generally tracks over the ocean, east of the mainland of Massachusetts. Because of its counterclockwise circulation, the nor'easter — as New Englanders pronounce it—creates large storm waves that batter east-northeast-facing shores, such as Duxbury Beach.

Northeasters generally occur during fall, winter, and early spring months. High storm winds create steep waves that erode sand from the beach and move it to the near-shore surf zone to form sand bars. The sand is not lost but simply relocated. That is why the beach appears to have much more cobble in the winter and early spring—not because there are more rocks but rather less sand. With the frequency of winter storms, the sand generally remains in the near-shore sand bars all winter and early spring.

About mid-spring, storm frequency lessens, and the more quiescent ocean environment now changes the wave shape to a less steep form. These gentler waves move the sand landward, and by mid-summer the sand washes on shore to create an enjoyable, sandy beach. The summer winds blow the smaller sand grains landward to form dunes. The dune vegetation and snow fencing help trap sand to build the dunes higher and wider. The dunes in turn provide important wildlife habitat, and during the upcoming winter months protect the mainland from storm waves.

New England is affected less frequently by hurricanes (winds greater than 72 miles per hour) because colder ocean water in this region diminishes wind energy as a hurricane approaches. Most hurricanes that *pass through Massachusetts travel west of Buzzards Bay. The counterclockwise circulation, which produces southeasterly winds, primarily affects the south shore of Cape Cod and the western shore of Buzzards Bay. Once the eye of a hurricane passes Duxbury Beach along its northward journey, the winds hitting the shore shift direction and begin to blow from the northwest. Although southeasterly and northwesterly winds of hurricane speed can cause catastrophic damage on the mainland, they are not as harmful to the beach as northeasters.*

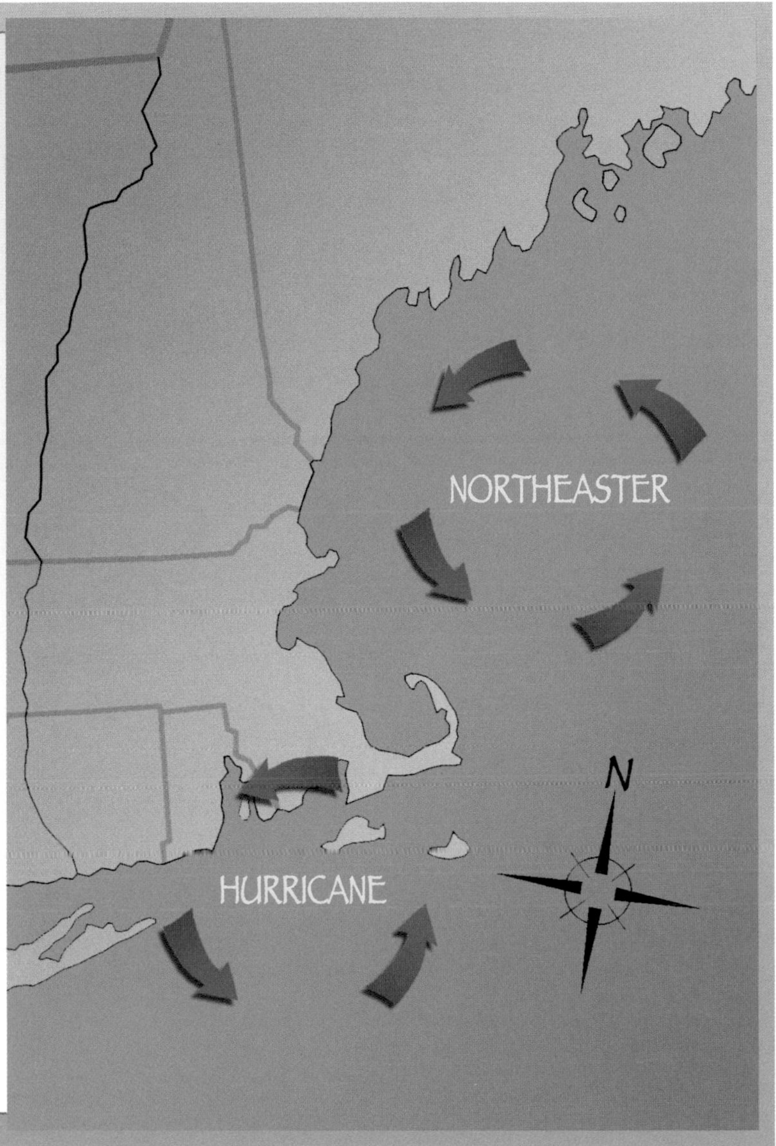

The Portland Gale

The Portland Gale, so named because of the loss of the luxury overnight steamer the *Portland*, was a double storm—the merger of a well-predicted huge, cold depression sweeping in from the Great Lakes with a small, warm, moist depression that was all but invisible to weather watchers as it raced up the Atlantic coast. Far more violent than the mere sum of its parts, the coastal storm packed winds reaching almost 90 knots (about 104 miles per hour). From New York to eastern Maine, it halted train and ferry service, tore up harbors, set ocean liners and lightships adrift, and wrecked or disabled at least 350 vessels. The storm and its accompanying blizzard killed more Americans in 36 hours than died in three months of combat during the recently completed Spanish-American War.

The best-known tragedy of the storm was the *Portland*, a steamer that departed from Boston at 7 P.M. on November 26, 1898,

Timeline

1871 – U.S. Lighthouse Service erects Duxbury Pier "Bug" Light on ledge off Saquish Point. Duxbury and Cohasset railroad opens; Myles Standish Monument ground-breaking ceremony takes place.

September 30, 1871 – Voters at Duxbury town meeting approve an article to sell the beach.

1871 1871

A view of the beach from the Powder Point Bridge after the Portland Gale of 1898.

crowded with passengers returning home to Portland, Maine, after the Thanksgiving holiday. At the time of her departure, the weather was threatening but had not yet deteriorated to the point that sailing was deemed inadvisable. Conditions quickly worsened, however. At 9:30 P.M. the *Portland* was sighted passing Thatcher's Island, a short distance northeast of Boston, her progress clearly hampered by the severe weather. Although she was reported to be making headway against the storm, she probably did not get much farther before her progress was halted.

To save his vessel, Captain Blanchard tried to head out to sea to weather the storm. He turned east, but the storm carried him southeast. The *Portland* was off Cape Cod in the morning. The eye of the storm passed over the Cape at about 9:00 A.M. and soon enveloped the *Portland*, now struggling to stay afloat. The wind then shifted 180 degrees to the northwest and continued at the same velocity, resulting in a wildly turbulent sea. The best guess as to what happened next is that a rogue wave tore the deck off the 280-foot sidewheeler (so-called because the steamer had a massive overhanging structure that housed her paddlewheels), and she went down with 192 people on board.

Duxbury Beach was in the center of the worst of the storm, which destroyed the east end of the Powder Point Bridge as it devastated the beach. There were serious wash-throughs (breaches caused by ocean water cutting through the dunes and pouring into the bay) all along the beach, and the vegetation on the beach was all but obliterated. A high water mark engraved on the stone wall in front of the King Caesar house shows that the water in the bay was higher in 1898 than in 1991 during the No-Name Storm.

The Portland Gale of 1898 is best remembered because of the lives lost when the *Portland* sank. But it was also a decisive event in the history of Duxbury Beach because it convinced William Wright, a local developer and owner of the beach, to give up his plans of building hundreds of cottages on the beach. Photographs from the time attest

Close Call for the *Pavonia*

A major disaster was narrowly averted off Duxbury Beach in October 1886 during a severe northeaster. The Cunard ocean liner Pavonia *was bound from Liverpool, England, to Boston with 400 passengers and 100 crew members on board when it ran aground on High Pines Ledge, a shoal of rocks about a mile off High Pines.*

The lifesaving crew from the Gurnet Life-Saving Station spotted the ship and launched a rescue boat, despite the heavy surf on the beach. They encountered a boat coming from the liner whose crew was "very ungentlemanly" and who only wanted to be taken to Plymouth to telegraph Boston. In the meantime, the liner, which for some reason was headed south, away from Boston, backed off the ledge and tore two holes in its side.

The Pavonia *then proceeded south toward Manomet, headed directly toward White Horse Beach in the thick mist. The lifesaving crew from the Manomet station reached the* Pavonia *only to find that the captain of the ship thought he was north of Boston, not south. He blamed his mistake on the whistling buoy off the Gurnet, which he mistook for one off Boston.*

Although his ship was taking on a lot of water, the captain decided to turn the huge liner around and make a run for Boston. By the time the ship reached Boston Light, its compartments were so full of water that the ship's bow was deep under water and its stern above water. Despite the darkness and high winds, all the passengers were transferred down ladders and safely into boats that brought them to shore. Plymouth's Old Colony Memorial *newspaper called it "the narrowest escape from a fearful disaster that ever occurred in the bay."*

Emergency repairs were made on the Pavonia *before she sailed back to Liverpool for full repairs. Yet it was only due to the crews from the Gurnet and Manomet Life-Saving Stations that the* Pavonia *averted the same fate that the* Portland *suffered twelve years later.*

Timeline

1872

1878

February 15, 1872 – The town of Duxbury sells the beach to Stephen M. Allen for $3,100. Allen forms Duxbury Bridge and Beach Company with his partners, Duxbury residents Stephen Gifford and John Loring.

1878 – First Gurnet Life-Saving Station is built.

Recollection of the Portland Gale

James Killian lived at the end of Fort Hill Avenue (now Lane) during the great storm of 1898 when the steamer Portland *foundered. Mr. Killian's daughter Gertrude Clement relates in a letter she wrote in 1938 how her father had removed the middle section of the house, which used to be a long rambling boarding house for mill hands, and relocated it along the shore near the mouth of the Blue Fish River. She writes: "We were living in the shore cottage when the* Portland *went down and my daughter was two years old. The house was entirely surrounded by water during the tidal wave and we found small fish frozen on the piazza floor."*

to the severity of the storm, and interestingly, show that damage to the beach in 1898 was strikingly similar to the damage from the Blizzard of '78 and the No-Name Storm.

The Blizzard of '78

Duxbury Beach took a terrible beating from the Blizzard of 1978, the worst storm to hit the beach since the Portland Gale. The blizzard caused 26 major wash-throughs. One of these breaches, just south of Plum Hills, was 1,200 feet wide. A second one, just north of High Pines, measured 2,000 feet in width.

In addition to the major wash-throughs, there were numerous washovers (partial breaches) where the waves broke through the dunes but did not carry sediment into the bay. Two of these occurred at the main resident parking lot. Although the sand and stones did not wash into the bay, they covered the parking lot with deposits 2 to 3 feet deep.

The damage to the dunes adjacent to the town parking lots was less than in other locations, due to conservation efforts over the previous ten years. Snow fencing and beach grass protected the dunes and reduced the destruction considerably. Damage was limited to 10 to 15 feet of erosion on the ocean side of the dunes. However, north of the main parking lot and south of the restored area, where no fencing had been installed or beach grass planted, the damage to the dunes was severe.

In many areas, the beach road to Gurnet and Saquish was completely obliterated. To reestablish the road and repair the dunes, bulldozers brought back more than 45,000 cubic yards of sand and stone that had washed onto the flats and marshes on the bay side. The Duxbury Beach Reservation installed approximately 15,500 feet of snow fence and many thousand feet of post and cable fence along the dunes and roadway. Beside the town parking lot, volunteers planted beach grass to stabilize the remaining dunes. The restoration work was accomplished just in time to withstand another major storm in January of the following year. Although substantial, the damage inflicted by the 1979 storm was

An aerial view of the town resident parking lot after the Blizzard of '78. Sand, stone, and snow fencing cover the lot, leaving only a few posts where the dunes once were.

Looking north from the beach entrance after the Blizzard of '78. The beach grass held the dune sand, but the fencing was ripped apart.

September 11, 1884 – Stephen M. Allen, Stephen W. Gifford, and John S. Loring sell the beach to Florentine W. Pelton of Dedham for $4,500.

1886 – Executors of Florentine Pelton's estate sell the beach to Arthur F. Mansur.

1887 – Arthur F. Mansur sells the beach to George Wright.

Timeline

1884 1886 1887

At right: Newly planted dunes in April 1974 south of the beach entrance.

Far right: After the 1991 No-Name Storm, the beach south of the first vehicle crossover was devastated. The right-of-way road disappeared along with the post and cable fencing. All that remained were the stubs of the posts.

mild compared to the Blizzard of '78.

The restoration program following the Blizzard of '78 was based on the theory that dunes build naturally from sand collected from the east, even though the beach itself is slowly moving westward. Therefore, the Reservation placed a row of snow fence 8

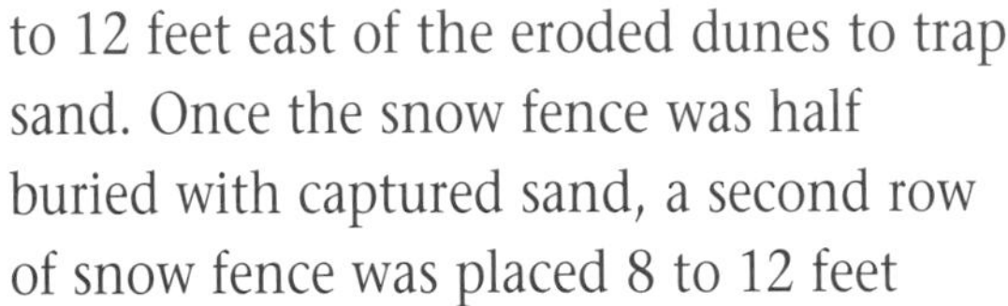

to 12 feet east of the eroded dunes to trap sand. Once the snow fence was half buried with captured sand, a second row of snow fence was placed 8 to 12 feet east of the first row. Beach grass was planted between and in front of the fences.

This procedure had recreational implications, however. For example, when a new row of snow fence was installed, it reduced the area of beach available for beach goers during high tide. Nevertheless, from 1978 to 1991, the Reservation added a row of fence every two or three years. Success was measured by comparing the width and height of the dunes with baseline measurements from 1973. For example, in 1973, the dunes in front of the town parking lot were 45 to 50 feet wide at the entrance to the beach and 60 to 75 feet wide at the north end of the parking lot. After the Blizzard of '78, these dunes decreased in width by 10 to 15 feet. By the time of the No-Name Storm in 1991, the dunes had increased in width

to 116 feet at the beach entrance and 180 feet at the north end of the lot, more than double the 1973 measurements. The height of the dunes increased from 3 to 6 feet over the entire area. South of the beach entrance, the dunes had grown 12 to 15 feet high.

Most of these restoration efforts were undone by the No-Name Storm. However, one can only imagine how much worse the damage would have been without the restoration work that followed the Blizzard of '78.

The No-Name Storm[1]

The so-called No-Name, or Halloween, Storm of Wednesday and Thursday, October 30 and 31, 1991—more recently referred to as "The Perfect Storm" after Sebastian Junger's best-selling book—was unexpected, unannounced, and unforeseen by most people. Those involved with Duxbury Beach and Duxbury Harbor, however, were well aware of the impending storm and braced for the worst when they observed the mud flats in the bay covered by an ominous half-tide at low tide.

Unusual conditions, almost identical to those of the Portland Gale, made this storm ferocious and damaging. A northeaster collided with former hurricane Grace near Cape Sable Island off of Nova Scotia and then turned 150 degrees to the southeast, almost directly toward Duxbury Beach. The force of the combined storms created very heavy and continuously building seas for a long period, making the No-Name Storm one of the most devastating that the south coastal beaches of Massachusetts have experienced in modern times.

Although the general public was unaware of the magnitude of the storm, residents of the Gurnet and Saquish had seen debris coming over the beach for two days before the storm hit. When the broken-down hurricane and northeaster combined, they triggered dangerous washovers of Duxbury Beach, severely damaged homes in Green Harbor, and panicked those stranded on the Gurnet and Saquish.

Sometime early on Wednesday, October 30, lobsterman Bill Bennett and harbormaster Don Beers were horrified to see that some washovers had already

Timeline

1891 1892 1895

1891 – Duxbury Rural and Historical Society acquires its first property, beginning a tradition of land conservation in Duxbury.

1892 – William A. Kenrick & Sons of East Boston begin construction of Gurnet Bridge (Powder Point Bridge). Second Gurnet Life-Saving Station is built.

1895 – Gurnet Bridge is completed and opening ceremonies take place.

A front-end loader frees Geoff Nudd's truck from the sand on the Friday following the No-Name Storm.

occurred. They were on the beach to guide a sailor in a 32-foot sailboat, who was desperately trying to reach safety in Plymouth Harbor. He was being watched by each town's harbormaster from Boston to Plymouth as he went by. Bennett and Beers watched helplessly as the boat almost capsized at High Pines Ledge before somehow righting itself. They guided the sailor around Gurnet Point to a Plymouth harbormaster's boat waiting near Bug Light. The sailor suffered only a broken arm.

Early in the afternoon of that same day, while on his way from work in Marshfield to his home on the Gurnet, Geoff Nudd stopped on Gurnet Road to check on a friend with a new baby. Although he stopped to warn the family away from the dangerous ocean and back onto the mainland, he felt secure enough himself to head down the beach in his pickup. The water was up to the floorboards of his truck, but Nudd continued along where he thought the road should be. Suddenly, an enormous wave knocked his truck on its side, and he scrambled to get out. He watched as huge storm waves broke through and carved a deep gully very near his truck. Panicked that he would get caught in the undertow, he first sought shelter in the truck but then struggled on foot through heavy waters and material "like quicksand," eventually making his way to Patrick and Colin Cudmore's cottage in the hollow of High Pines.

Nudd was black and blue from being tossed among boulders in the surf and severely hypothermic from the cold October water. The Cudmores stripped off his wet clothes and placed him in their bathtub filled with warm water to raise his body temperature. He gradually recovered in a sleeping bag, in front of the fire. Outside, the storm continued to rage, sending waves over 90 percent of the beach and even dumping torrents of water into the hollow at High Pines.

Not long after that, firefighter Wayne Sjostedt, after responding to a house fire alarm on Gurnet Road near Cable Hill, set out on foot toward the pavilion parking lot. He watched in horror as a wall of water 5 to 6 feet high crashed into the retaining wall near him. It created

The First Look

The infamous No-Name Storm of October 30 and 31, 1991, was still raging, but the winds were slowly abating. It was late afternoon on Thursday, October 31, when I received a call from Harbormaster Don Beers, asking me to join him and Conservation Commissioner Shawn Dahlen to make a brief survey of the beach. We approached the beach from Gurnet Road because the Powder Point Bridge was still too dangerous.

We entered the pavilion parking lot through the main gate and into the overflow parking lot by the main gate but could go no further. The road was covered with a soupy mess of sand and water. I waded through the muck to the main parking lot. The large dune that protects the parking area was intact for 100 yards from the north. Beyond there, it looked like a knife had cut the dune at an oblique angle—the rest of the dune to the south was completely gone, having spread all over the parking lot.

Shawn had checked the pavilion and returned to report that the lunchroom was severely damaged. By now it was obvious that the beach had suffered serious damage. The road was so bad that our four-wheel drive truck could not go forward or in reverse. Don called for help and we were pulled clear by a town vehicle.

The next morning after the storm had passed, we crossed over the Powder Point Bridge and were able to view the enormity of the damage the beach had suffered. It was far worse than the great blizzard of 1978.

Al Krahmer, Vice President,
Duxbury Beach Reservation, Inc., 1991.

Timeline

1897 — Death of George Wright, first husband of Georgianna B. Wright.

November 27, 1898 — The Portland Gale causes several breaks in the beach and leaves the east end of the bridge hanging in mid-air; the luxury steamer *Portland* goes down off of Cape Cod, with 192 people on board.

1897 1898

a huge gully in the sand and carried him in his heavy firefighting gear—feet first, bobbing in 3 feet of water—into the parking lot. Luckily, a fellow firefighter was able to grab him before he was swept onto the marsh.

Meanwhile, the beach itself was fighting for its very existence. Anxious watchers on Cable Hill and Powder Point could see the peril. After almost two days of pounding against the beach, the sea had broken through the dunes and into the bay in eight or ten places, and the entire beach was under water at peak high tide. Shawn Dahlen, a conservation commissioner at the time, noted that with the exception of High Pines and Plum Hills, the entire beach was washed over; fencing and signage was carried into the bay, 90 to 95 percent of the vegetation was lost, and every primary dune was gone.

Al Krahmer, vice president of the Duxbury Beach Reservation at the time, was convinced that the storm was five to eight times worse than the Blizzard of '78.

Krahmer quickly called in Fred Nava, a local contractor, to assess the damage. Nava had grown up on Saquish, knew the beach, and had played a major role in building the back road to the Gurnet and Saquish. After a brief survey of the devastation, Krahmer and Nava agreed that the first priority was to fill in the major breaches and open the road.

On Friday, November 1, a meeting was held at Duxbury's town offices. Bob Fuchs, a representative of Massachusetts Coastal Zone Management, was present, along with Krahmer, Nava, Dahlen and other town, state, and federal officials. Fuchs asked what was needed to rebuild Duxbury Beach. Before anyone could speak, Dahlen asked for "a dozen D-8s" (large model Caterpillar bulldozers). Fuchs promised to see what he could do and before day's end called to say that the U.S. Army Corps of Engineers would have the necessary earth-moving equipment on the beach Saturday morning.

As promised, at 8:00 A.M. Saturday, 20 bulldozers and front-end loaders assembled in the town parking lot. The Reservation placed Nava in charge of the operators and equipment, and the restoration efforts began in earnest. The crews labored 12 hours a day to move huge "noses" of sand out of the bay and into the breaches. Then they started work on rebuilding the road. "They told me to put it back together—so I did," said Nava.

The damage to the beach was extreme. High Pines survived, but the dunes south of High Pines suffered serious damage. In fact, most of the dunes from High Pines to Plum Hills were destroyed and washed onto the marsh on the west side of the beach. The Plum Hills section had boasted the largest dunes on the beach, vegetated with both shrubs and trees. While it was not totally overwashed by the storm, Plum Hills did suffer two serious breaches that threatened the integrity of the beach at that point. Another major breach occurred south of the first vehicle crossover where water at high tide surged from the ocean into the bay. This breach was the first one to be repaired in order to prevent a major break in the beach.

A fleet of large bulldozers arrived on the beach after the No-Name Storm to begin the massive restoration effort.

Bulldozers moved huge "noses" of sand from the bay and pushed them back into the dunes to close the breaches.

1898 – Myles Standish Monument is completed.

1900 – William J. Wright, nephew of George Wright, marries Georgianna B. Wright.

May 27, 1902 – Georgianna B. Wright becomes owner of Duxbury Beach.

Timeline 1898 1900 1902

The Role of Woody Vegetation

In the early 1970s, extensive grass planting took place along Duxbury Beach. Although the grass grew very well in sandy areas, it did not do well in eroded areas behind the dunes where beach buggy trails did not fill up with wind-deposited sand. Members of the Duxbury Beach Association and the Duxbury Beach Reservation had noted that several species of woody vegetation thrived in the back dunes. Among them were salt-spray roses, beach plum, and bayberry. These plants had demonstrated for decades a unique ability to establish and maintain vigorous, isolated stands and dense thickets of vegetation.

Following the hints dropped and clues left by natural succession and forces at work on the beach, the managers undertook a modest experiment. Volunteers planted several dozen salt spray roses at several locations along the beach. All of these plants survived, and many remain today, rigorously testifying to the success of those first efforts to establish woody vegetation on Duxbury Beach.

During the restoration efforts following the Blizzard of '78, the Reservation noted the durability of the woody vegetation. Unless it had been completely uprooted or washed out, beach plum, salt spray roses, and bayberry were clinging to life by roots that remained anchored in the sand and gravel. Specimens buried by overwashed sand and gravel responded vigorously, with new vegetative growth, flowers, and fruit. The same thing happened after the No-Name Storm. To this date, many of the sites restored support survivors of both storms coexisting with additional plants introduced after the storms.

Richmond Poole, trustee, Duxbury Beach Reservation, Inc.

Left: Sand from the dunes south of High Pines spreads over the salt marshes to the west during the No-Name Storm.

Above: A close look at one of the wash-throughs at Plum Hills.

It took weeks for the Reservation to remove approximately 400,000 cubic yards of sand from the bay, the salt marshes, and the parking lots and return it to the dune areas. Removing sand from the salt marshes was particularly difficult. The Massachusetts Department of Environmental Protection feared that the marsh would be irreparably damaged if heavy equipment were employed. Therefore, only a small wide-track bulldozer was used to painstakingly remove sand from the marshes.

After the emergency repair work, the dune profile of Duxbury Beach was still so low that the Federal Emergency Management Agency (FEMA) agreed to pay 75 percent of the $1,167,741 cost to return the dunes to their pre-storm height of 16½ feet. To do this, the Reservation brought in almost 58,000 cubic yards of compatible quarry sand. New snow fencing was installed, and volunteers planted 500,000 culms of beach grass to stabilize the artificial dune.

The safety of the people living on the Gurnet and Saquish was a major factor in the initial rapid response of the state and federal agencies. Continued support by the agencies was due to the

Timeline

1909 1912 1913 1919

1909 – The new brick library given by the Wright family is dedicated.

1912 – Death of William J. Wright.

1913 – First attempt by the state to take Duxbury Beach.

1919 – Death of Georgianna B. Wright.

November 6, 1919 – Estate of Georgianna Wright sells beach to Frederick S. Pratt for $15,000.

By June 1992, the town resident parking lot had been repaved, and the snow fencing had been replaced on the east side of the dunes, the walkways, and the beach entrance.

effective work of the team under Fred Nava's capable direction. In fact, certain agencies were so impressed with the reconstruction team's dedication and quality work that they authorized days of work far beyond the initial commitment.

Once the beach was safe from wash-throughs and the back road to the Gurnet and Saquish was repaired and passable, the government agencies left the detailed mending to the Reservation to complete. By the following autumn, the beach was essentially restored to its pre-storm condition, although a severe northeaster in December 1992 undid much of the restoration work. The team went to work again, and finally, by 1994, the beach was in fair shape.

Mother Nature has been comparatively kind to the beach since the No-Name Storm, but the caretakers of Duxbury Beach remain vigilant in doing everything possible under current regulations to protect the beach from the next great storm.

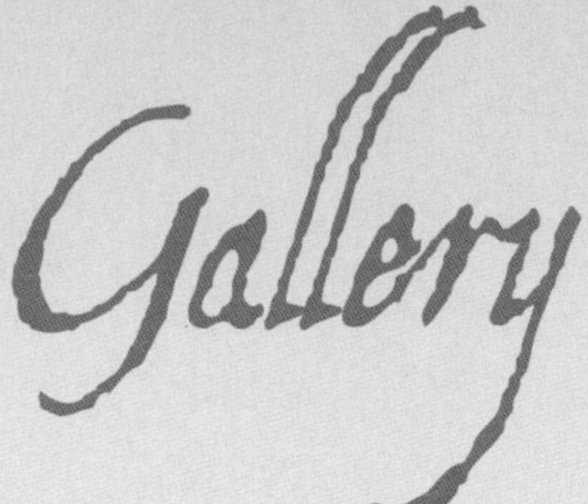

Gallery

The Portland Gale of 1898. The top photo (looking south) shows one of the several breaches caused by the storm. The Wright cottages can be seen in the distance. In the left photo, the Powder Point Bridge, only three years old when the storm struck, was severely damaged.

Gallery

A closeup of the photo on page 60 shows that the east end of the bridge washed away during the Portland Gale.

Two early postcards, c. 1905, show large chunks of ice along Duxbury Beach during a particularly severe New England winter.

An enormous tree on Clark's Island toppled in the 1944 hurricane. Clint Watson is the boy in the tree.

Gallery

Above: Looking north along Duxbury Beach after the Blizzard of '78. Only the fence posts remain, far in front of the dunes that used to be there.

Left: Looking north along Duxbury Beach from the main entrance after the No-Name Storm. The damage bears a strong resemblance to the damage from the '78 storm.

Six houses once stood on Reservation land north of the pavilion parking lot. Three were lost during the Blizzard of '78 and two more during the No-Name Storm. Today, only the cottage on the far right remains.

The No-Name Storm destroyed the pavilion lunch room. The main structure received only minor damage.

6

DUXBURY BEACH...

Stewards of the Beach

Duxbury Beach Association, 1919–1975

The future course of Duxbury Beach was determined in 1919 when the estate of Georgianna Wright offered the property for sale. In order to prevent further real estate speculation, a small group of summer residents, led by Frederick S. Pratt, raised $15,000 through subscriptions of $100 per share and purchased the beach from its northernmost end at Rouse's Hummock and Pine Point, south to the Plymouth line. They took title as the Duxbury Beach Association with the declared objective "to preserve Duxbury Beach against encroachments detrimental to Powder Point and the Town of Duxbury."[1]

Before long, the Association also assumed responsibility for providing parking for residents at the east end of the bridge and for the public at the north end of the beach. Pratt, later assisted and then succeeded by his son, Frederick T. Pratt, was the man chiefly responsible for conceiving and carrying out these objectives. It was only through the foresight and actions of the Association that Duxbury Beach did not become another Coney Island.

A view of Gurnet Creek looking north toward Clark's Island and Duxbury.

Timeline

1919

1920

1922

November 29, 1919 – Frederick S. Pratt transfers beach title to Duxbury Beach Association, a common law trust.

1920 – State attempts to take the beach.

December 9, 1922 – Massachusetts Land Court confirms Duxbury Beach Association's title to the southerly 3.5 miles of beach.

The Association operated the beach from 1919 until 1975. It was, from start to finish, an act of pure philanthropy. The trustees served without compensation, and no dividends were ever paid on the shares. To ensure they would have a direct interest in Duxbury, shareholders had to own property in the town. When a shareholder died or sold his property in Duxbury, the Association bought back the shares.

Before the Association could take full control of the beach, however, it had to deal with the presence of squatters' shacks and gunning stands. By refusing to acknowledge the Association's ownership or to pay rent, many of the squatters were gradually acquiring title to the land. This forced the Association to apply to the state Land Court for registered title. With assistance from real estate agent Percy L. Walker, a settlement was soon reached with the few squatters and gunning-stand occupants on the southern 3½ miles of the beach, and the Association received registered title to that section in 1922.

The northern portion of the property was more complicated. Besides having to purchase marshland bordering the beach in order to clarify property lines, the Association had to confront 20 squatters who owned cottages on the northerly half mile of the beach. Many of these squatters refused to pay rent for the land on which their cottages stood; however, the Association had to pay real estate taxes on the cottages. The Association again applied to the Land Court for relief. At first, the squatters refused to settle, but when it became clear that a local fisherman who lived year-round on the beach was going to lose his case, most of them decided to come to an agreement with the Association.

To expedite the settlements, the Association provided land to which the squatters' houses could be moved. For that purpose, Pine Point, a part of the original purchase located at the northernmost end of the beach, was chosen and lots were laid out and priced. Squatters were offered three- to five-year leases on the land under their houses or, if they chose to move their houses, the opportunity to buy one of the Pine Point lots for $100 less than the asking price.[2] In 1932, the Land Court issued a final decree, at last granting the Association full registered title to the entire 4-mile stretch of beach it had purchased 13 years earlier.

The Association barely had time to savor its victory before a three-day northeaster struck in January 1933, covering the parking lots with a foot of sand and rocks and carrying a squatter's house—just purchased by the Association for $100—out to sea. To repair the beach in the wake of the storm, damaged material removed from the bridge was constructed into a fence to act as a "sand catcher," which was effective for several years until it was demolished in a major storm.

Financing the operations of the Association, including beach preservation, land purchases, taxes, insurance, legal costs, and repurchase of shares, was never easy. The bulk of the Association's earnings from 1920 to 1931 came from rentals of gunning stands, but beginning in 1935 restrictions on shooting Canada geese became so severe that many gunning stands remained vacant. By 1942 no revenue at all was received from the gunning stands.

Daniel Webster: Orator, Beach Protector

Daniel Webster, the famous Massachusetts statesman and antebellum-era debater, had a role in early attempts to control erosion on Duxbury Beach. According to Frederick S. Pratt, "I understand it to be a fact that [in 1832] Daniel Webster obtained a $30,000 grant from Congress for construction of a barrier consisting of two layers of heavy wooden planks [actually a double line of fences with stakes driven into the ground] with eel grass stuffed between. For many years this was completely covered by sand, but now it shows in a number of places on the Beach."

Records of Duxbury Beach Association, Vol. 2, p. 164.

Storms and finances were not the only problems. Bills in the state legislature calling for state ownership of beaches were also a constant worry for the Association. In fact, the state had eyed Duxbury Beach as a potential eminent domain target as early as 1913. Bills were filed every couple of years, but the most serious challenges arose in 1929, 1950, and 1969. Partly as a response to the 1929 threat and partly to resolve traffic problems, the town of Duxbury and the Association trustees agreed in 1931 that the Association would provide two

Timeline

1923-1926 – Duxbury Beach Association purchases marshes adjoining Duxbury Beach.

1924 – North tower of the Gurnet Lighthouse is taken down.

January 20, 1926 – Duxbury Beach Association sells the three Wright cottages to Walter G. Prince for $1,500 cash, for removal prior to June 1, 1926.

FREDERICK S. PRATT
1873–1968

It is to Frederick S. Pratt, more than any other person, that we owe the state of Duxbury Beach today. When the estate of Georgianna Wright offered the property for sale, Pratt formed a coalition of summer residents to buy the beach and protect it on behalf of the town. Because the Duxbury Beach Association was not yet formalized by the November 6, 1919, closing date, Pratt took title in his own name, transferring ownership to the Association 23 days later. As chairman of the Association trustees, he worked out the complex and delicate real estate and legal transactions that gradually cleared the beach of cottages. He managed the rentals, leases, and sales that financed beach operations, the construction of parking lots, and the purchase of bordering marshlands; or when receipts were insufficient, issued additional shares in the Association. In 1935, he transferred lands he owned on Gurnet and Saquish to the Association for minimal consideration. He kept a watchful eye on the State House, and led negotiations with state representatives, county commissioners, and town officials, all of whom had designs on the beach. After holding the position for more than 30 years, Pratt retired as chairman in 1950, but continued to serve as a trustee until two weeks before his death in 1968 at the age of 95. His carefully detailed records, preserved in the Duxbury library, document his remarkable legacy.

parking areas: a resident lot at the east end of the bridge and Duxbury Beach Park, a separate, public lot at the north end of the beach. For its part, the town would extend Gurnet Road to provide access through Marshfield to the public lot. It would also police both lots and prohibit parking on the bridge and town roads. The public lot was leased to T. Waldo Herrick, with the understanding that the Association would receive a share of the parking receipts.

In 1941, the Association constructed a new public lot at Duxbury Beach Park, improved the roads, and built the pavilion. Additional shares in the Association were sold to finance the improvements. In his annual report to the trustees, F. S. Pratt wrote, with his usual prescience, "While the active entry of this country into the war and particularly the curtailment of motoring may prove the investment to have been premature, nevertheless we accomplished our purpose of meeting public demand for improved facilities…"[3]

World War II affected everyone and everything, not the least Duxbury Beach. With gas rationed, driving was reduced to a minimum. People could not get to the beach easily, and revenues from parking fell drastically; Herrick did not operate the pavilion and public lot at all during the summers of 1944 and 1945. Meanwhile, in 1942 the Association granted rights of beach access to the federal government so the U.S. Army could guard the coast. Trenches were dug, gun emplacements were built, and practice maneuvers were conducted on the beach. After the war, the town proposed acquiring the beach as a war memorial, but after two years of discussions, the project was dropped.

Germany and Japan surrendered in 1945, but Mother Nature remained a formidable foe. On November 29, the sea swept over almost the whole beach south of the bridge, creating new beaches on the bay side by burying beach grass under sand. F. S. Pratt recorded his general impression "that the beach has been somewhat flattened as a whole, and that it has moved bodily toward the shore…"[4] Another battle loomed when the 1949 session of the Massachusetts legislature brought forward a bill for the acquisition of four beaches, including Duxbury Beach. Underlying this and similar bills was the state's position that the growth of private beaches was increasingly restricting public rights of access, that of 800 miles of beaches in Massachusetts only 17 were controlled by the state, and that immediate action was imperative. The Association countered that with the pavilion building and parking spaces now for 600 cars, the public was adequately served by the facilities at Duxbury Beach Park, and the 30-year record of its present ownership was assurance that the beach would always remain open to the public.

Two separate bills filed in 1950 brought the situation to a head. It was the first challenge for Frederick T. "Ted" Pratt, who had just replaced his father as chairman of the trustees. A determined alliance of the Association trustees, town officials, the Duxbury Citizens' Protest Committee, and opposition groups

1928 – State attempts to take the beach.

1929 – State attempts to take the beach.

1931 – Duxbury Beach Association builds a parking lot for Duxbury residents at the east end of the bridge and a public lot for non-residents at the north end of the beach; hires T. Waldo Herrick to manage public lot.

Timeline

1928 1929 1931

representing other beaches managed to defeat both bills. The continual threat of state takeover, however, prompted town meeting to appoint a committee to study the question of town versus private ownership. The committee's report concluded that private ownership by the Association was advantageous to the town, and that a state taking depended more on how the beach was operated than whether it was publicly or privately owned. The committee did suggest that the Association, still made up entirely of summer residents, invite some year-round residents to become trustees. Harry Bradley, a former selectman and town moderator, and Thomas W. Herrick, son of the first operator of Duxbury Beach Park, were appointed soon after.

Hurricane Carol struck on August 31, 1954, severely damaging the pavilion and the bridge. But it was people in "beach buggies"—four-wheel-drive jeeps or cars with balloon tires—driving wherever they liked, creating cuts through the dunes, killing beach grass and other vegetation, who were now the greatest threat to the beach.

Concerned that uncontrolled recreational use was seriously degrading the dunes, the Association asked the 1959 town meeting to approve $800 for a summer police patrol on the beach, but the money was turned down.

It took only two years for town meeting voters to change their minds. With deterioration of the beach becoming impossible to ignore, they approved $4,500 for a summer police patrol after the Association offered to provide a jeep. The patrol worked well, and voters in subsequent years continued to approve funding for the summer police. Some of the town's cost was offset by the sale of parking stickers. Residents were charged $1 for a permit, and beginning in 1964 non-residents could buy a $2 permit to park on the beach itself. That year the town sold 2,466 resident stickers and 323 non-resident stickers.

Litter on the beach was another problem. In what became an annual event, volunteers organized a cleanup in 1962. This was the first manifestation of an increasing interest in the beach and participation in its management by groups of people not affiliated with the Association. Shortly after the cleanups were initiated, volunteers inspired and led by Duxbury resident John Nash began trying to deter erosion. To prevent vehicles from cutting across the dunes and to trap sand, they attached snow fencing to the Coast Guard telephone poles that ran all the way to the Gurnet. Beginning at the bridge and working south, they put up 800 feet of fence in 1964 and 1,000 feet in 1965. A year later, they began experimenting with Christmas trees to trap sand.

In another volunteer effort that has since become a tradition, Richmond Poole, whose graduate thesis at the Yale School of Forestry was the basis for many of the erosion control projects on Duxbury Beach, planted 15,000 culms of beach grass in 1973 with the help of 27 students. The next year 150 volunteers turned out to plant beach grass.

The trustees of the Association were meanwhile preoccupied with matters both personal and political. The former involved the appointment of Charles H. Wood as trustee in 1968 to replace Frederick S. Pratt, the last of the original trustees, who died two weeks later. The latter had to do with the state sanitary code. A seemingly innocent voluntary program of "minimum standards for

Pratt's Goose

When the Duxbury Beach Association took possession of the beach and the three Wright houses in 1919, there were a number of cottages and gunning stands on the beach belonging to others. While negotiating for the removal of the structures, the Association tried to collect lease payments from the owners. The effort met with success in a few cases but by no means all. Some potential confrontations were diffused with grace and humor, as Frederick S. Pratt described in his report to the Association trustees dated January 2, 1934.

> *On November 19th I found that a small shooting stand for geese had been erected by George Stetson on the beach a short distance north of the Dunn stand. I cautioned him against using Duxbury Beach property without a lease. He handed me a goose (a tough old bird) and, as I couldn't find a market in which to liquidate the goose, I bought it by paying the Duxbury Beach Association $1.00 and sent a permit to Stetson to maintain his stand throughout the shooting season. The total receipts for the 1933 shooting season were therefore $1001.00.*

Timeline

1931 – Town of Duxbury extends Gurnet Road to reach the entrance to the public parking lot.

May 14, 1932 – Massachusetts Land Court confirms Duxbury Beach Association's title to the northerly half mile of the beach.

January 26-28, 1933 – 3-day northeaster severely damages the beach and bridge.

"Blakeman's"

T. Waldo Herrick ran Duxbury Beach Park for 17 years, beginning in 1931. In 1947, his last year, he was assisted by Ralph N. Blakeman, a teacher at Duxbury High School. Mr. Blakeman proved a worthy successor to Mr. Herrick. According to Frederick S. Pratt in his January 2, 1948, report to the trustees, "Blakeman, with his wife and child, lived at the pavilion all summer and worked long hours and, I feel, very effectively. I think he will handle the work well; in fact, there is some danger that he may prove too able to remain interested in the job." It turned out that Ralph and Thelma Blakeman spent 38 years running Duxbury Beach Park, or "Blakeman's" as it became known. Gordon Leighton was concessionaire from 1985 through 2000, after which Dana and Missy Battista took over.

Duxbury Beach Park pavilion under construction in 1941.

bathing beaches" turned out to be yet another attempt to take beaches by eminent domain, with Duxbury Beach a primary target.

Besides being caught up in state politics, the trustees were simultaneously dealing with an extensive recreational operation, erosion problems, and continuing complaints about litter. They were also engaged in biological projects, including separate studies of small rodents and migratory shorebirds, and the setting aside of an area at High Pines for nesting least terns. It was a heavy burden for a shrinking volunteer organization, and the town stepped in to help.

A beach study committee appointed by the selectmen in 1972 produced a small booklet with an hourglass on the cover and the title "Duxbury—Where Sand is Running Out." The introduction began with the question, "Can you imagine Duxbury without Big Beach?" In response to the booklet, the 1973 town meeting voted $8,000 for a beach conservation officer and $12,000 for the first beach lease. The annual lease payment provided the Association with additional funds to help maintain and restore the beach.

Despite the new funds, the Association was running out of steam. By the time it had marked its 50th anniversary in 1969, all of the original shareholders and trustees were gone and the current trustees were beginning to look for a more permanent solution to ownership and management of the beach. After much deliberation, they ruled out donating the beach to Duxbury's Conservation Commission, and in 1973 they opened discussions with The Trustees of Reservations, a non-profit conservation trust dedicated to the preservation of Massachusetts properties with scenic, historic, and ecological value. It seemed like a perfect fit, but the trust declined to accept the beach.

With no further options, the trustees set about the complex task of liquidating Duxbury Beach Association and creating a new organization to which ownership of the beach and responsibility for its protection would be passed. The beach, valued by a real estate appraisal firm at $1,116,000,[5] would be given to the new organization. Only the liquid assets of the Association, $125,500, or $525 per share, would be used to pay those shareholders wishing to sell rather than donate their shares. At the closing, Robert G. Millar, treasurer of the newly formed Duxbury Beach Reservation, Inc., came with checks made out to each of the selling shareholders, and Ted Pratt transferred the Association's $125,500 to the Reservation. In effect, the Association paid itself, while the beach was gifted to the Reservation. After 55 years of successful operation, Duxbury Beach Association closed its books and relinquished stewardship of the beach.

1933 – Plymouth County Commissioners ask Duxbury Beach Association to transfer beach to the county.

1934 – Plymouth County Commissioners again ask Duxbury Beach Association for beach.

1934 – Frederick S. Pratt transfers title to 140 acres at the south end of the beach, including Gurnet Creek and marshes on Saquish, to Duxbury Beach Association.

1935 – State attempts to take the beach.

Timeline

1933 1934 1935

Gallery

Duxbury Beach Park in 1952. Ralph and Thelma Blakeman were the park managers for 38 years.

A hot, sunny day at Blakeman's in the early 1950s.

Gallery

Duxbury Beach Park was a popular summer destination in the late 1960s.

On a number of occasions, a road was proposed across the marshes of the Back River. This 1952 map shows a route from Duck Hill Road (off Route 3A) to Duxbury Beach Park.

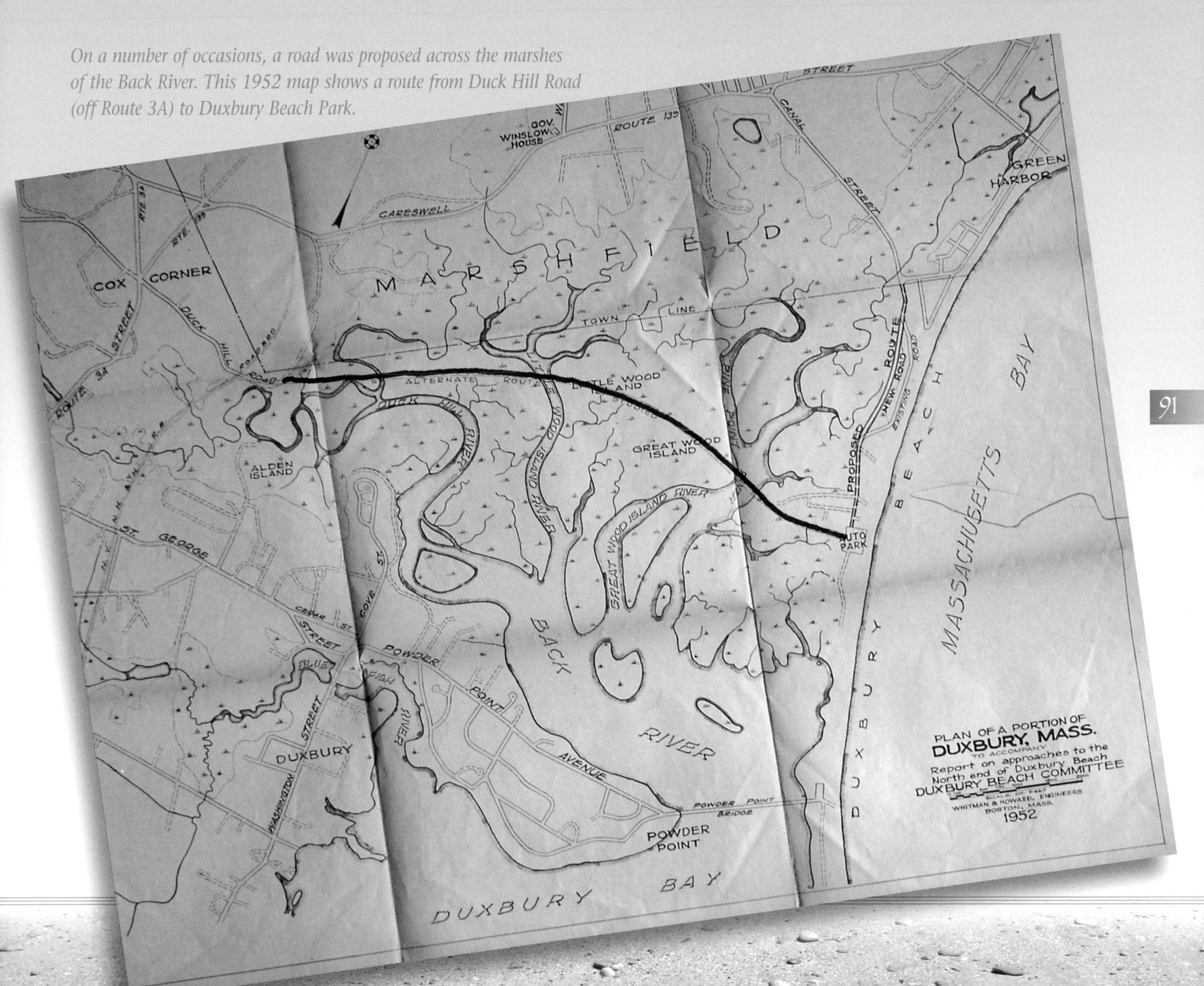

7 Duxbury Beach... Beyond the Beach

Gurnet, Saquish & Clark's Island

Samuel Adams Drake, in his 1875 book about the New England seacoast, wrote: *"[Duxbury Beach] terminates in a smaller pattern of the celebrated Italian boot. . . .The heel of the boot is toward the sea and called The Gurnet; the toe points landward, and is called Saquish Head. Just within the toe of the boot is Clark's Island, named [for] the master's mate of the Mayflower."*[1]

The Gurnet is a drumlin formed of glacial till deposited 20,000 years ago as the Wisconsin Glacier retreated northward from its southernmost point at Nantucket and Martha's Vineyard. Saquish Head and Clark's Island, also glacial drumlins, were once both islands, although a narrow strip of sand known as Saquish Neck now joins Saquish Head to the Gurnet.

The Gurnet, Saquish, and Clark's Island all became part of Plymouth Colony on January 7, 1638.[2] At first the lands were held in common, but in the 1690s they were sold to private individuals to defray town expenses. More than 350 years later they are still a part of Plymouth. The Plymouth-Duxbury town line runs in an east-west direction north of Clark's Island and across Duxbury Beach about half a

A view of Gurnet Point from Gurnet Creek

Timeline

1935

1936

1935 – Cost of building a direct-access road across the Back River marshes thwarts plan to make beach a State Reservation.

1936 – Duxbury Beach Association begins a scientific study of the beach and creates a "Beach Preservation Fund."

The artifact records of prehistoric occupation, some of which are pictured in the photos at right, include spear points and knives, scrapers and fishing weights (plummets), arrowheads, and a bone sewing awl, and are dated from 2500 B.C. to 500 A.D.

mile north of where the Gurnet guard shack now stands.

The Gurnet, Saquish, and Clark's Island are magical places. Located at the far end of Duxbury Beach and belonging to Plymouth, they are not really a part of either. They exist somewhere outside the twenty-first century, inhabited by a special breed of strong, self-reliant men and women, many of whom return summer after summer, generation after generation. There are no paved roads—no roads at all on Clark's Island. There are no public utilities, although generators, propane tanks, and solar panels have brought some modern conveniences, and indoor plumbing is now the norm. Just beyond the beach and only a few miles from civilization, the Gurnet, Saquish, and Clark's Island have the feel of another world and an earlier time when life was simpler.

The Gurnet

The Gurnet is small in size but rich in history, written and unwritten. Arrowheads and shells reveal the presence of

Native Americans over many centuries. While no one has positively dated the arrival of the first Europeans, artifacts suggest that Vikings may have visited the area a thousand years ago. The Norse sagas recount a voyage by Thorwald, son of Eric the Red, in 1004. Sailing in Cape Cod Bay, he landed on a wooded promontory so beautiful that he wanted to settle there. Instead, he was mortally wounded in a skirmish with natives and was buried there with crosses at his head and feet. The Vikings named the place "Krossaness." Some claim the hill was Point Allerton in Boston Harbor and some say Nahant, but many authorities believe it was the Gurnet.

More verifiable is the 1605 voyage of Pierre DuGua, Sieur de Monts, a merchant explorer sent by Henri IV to colonize for France the lands of North America between 40 and 60 degrees north latitude. He brought with him the royal cartographer, Samuel de Champlain, whose map of the area shows Clark's Island and Saquish as two separate islands within the arm of the Gurnet. Champlain's writings about the area describe the Gurnet as covered with pine trees, which would play a part in the settlement of the area.

Not long after the explorers came the Pilgrims, who, with their successors, valued the Gurnet, Saquish, and Clark's Island for their forests and other abundant resources. The early colonists came from Plymouth to gather wood or dig for clams, but around 1700 people began to live in these outlying areas. They farmed the rich upland soils and cut timber to build their homes and make masts for boats. They caught fish in the creeks and dug shellfish in the mudflats. They harvested salt marsh hay for their animals and manufactured salt on both the Gurnet and Clark's Island.

The upland area of the Gurnet is about 27 acres. Its name is believed to have been derived from gurnet fish, which were common along the coast of Devonshire, England; several headlands in the English Channel also bear the name Gurnet.

The first structure you see as you come onto the Gurnet from the beach is a building known as the "farmhouse." It was one of the first houses on the Gurnet, built of native timber by the Burgess family in about 1720. The Burgesses were among the earliest settlers on both the Gurnet and Saquish. They found the rich uplands to be productive for farming, and stone walls still mark the division of the fields they cleared. A large cow barn and chicken house, as well as several sheds, made for a very self-sufficient farm with a good well, which is still in use.

In 1872, George Hall of Marshfield bought the farm, enlarged the house to 20 rooms, made extensive improvements, moved a building from South Duxbury to serve as a dance pavilion, and ran the property as a summer inn for 13 years. Among the visitors were Joseph and Ellen Boardman of Boston. The Boardmans, neither the first nor the last people to fall in love with the Gurnet, traded their farm in Lexington for the Hall property in 1885. The Boardmans continued to operate the inn, which they called the Gurnet Inn, for 20 years.

1938 – Town of Duxbury agrees to assume control of bridge and full responsibility for maintenance costs.

1938 – The Great New England Hurricane causes breaches in several places along the beach.

1939 – End of Old Colony rail service to Duxbury.

Timeline 1938 1939

Delivering guests to the Gurnet Inn by oxcart, c. 1890.

Getting to the inn was a slow and uncomfortable 9-mile ride through Marshfield and down the beach. Guests rode in an oxcart, sitting on straight-backed kitchen chairs. When the Gurnet Bridge (Powder Point Bridge) opened in 1895, Mr. Boardman could pick up his guests at Duxbury's Millbrook Station instead of meeting them at the train station in Marshfield. The new bridge shortened the route to 6 miles, but it was still a slow journey. Some summer residents remember their fathers walking the 4 miles of beach on a Friday night after spending the workweek in Boston and taking the train to Millbrook Station.

In 1935, on the 50th anniversary of his grandparents' acquisition, Herbert Boardman wrote a history of the Gurnet and the inn, which was reprinted in a series of *Duxbury Clipper* articles beginning May 21, 1981. Based on his fond memories, sketches of local characters, and tales of high jinks at the inn, it is not surprising that several of the couples who came as guests later built or bought cottages of their own at the Gurnet.

Tomfoolery at the Boardmans'

"My family was there [at his grandparents' inn on the Gurnet in 1896] over 4th of July and it was probably on this Independence Day that my father had so much fun with his cannons. When it was time for the excursion steamer from Boston to round the point, he filled the cannon with old boots, overalls, and other riff-raff with which to salute the steamer. At the report of the cannon, Mrs. Holmes looked out the window in time to see these articles of clothing go flying through the air. She cried out in great excitement, 'The steamer has blown up and everyone has been blown to bits. There are arms and legs flying in the air everywhere!'"

Herbert Boardman, written in 1935 and reprinted in the *Duxbury Clipper*, June 18, 1981.

The Gurnet has a martial aspect as well. Commanding the entrance to Plymouth Harbor, Gurnet Point was a natural site for a fort. In 1776, the towns of Plymouth, Kingston, and Duxbury built Fort Andrew, an earthworks fort with a six-cannon battery. During the Revolutionary War, it was manned by militia from the three towns and engaged in skirmishes with British ships, including the 33-gun frigate, *H.M.S. Niger*. The *Niger*, which had run aground on Brown's Bank, fired its cannons and hit the lighthouse on the Gurnet, causing little damage but giving the lighthouse the distinction of being the only one ever hit by a cannon ball. Fort Andrew was rebuilt during the Civil War, and its earthen ramparts may still be clearly seen, both from the ground and in aerial photographs.

Crowning the Gurnet, and visible for miles in all directions, is the Gurnet Lighthouse. There may have been a primitive lighthouse as early as 1710, but in 1768 it was replaced by twin beacons, the first such light in America. Vessels going into Plymouth Harbor paid "light money" to help with the upkeep.

John Thomas, on whose land the light was built, was appointed the first lighthouse keeper. Thomas was a well-respected Kingston doctor who had served in the British Army and was known as a brilliant tactician, which is why George Washington called upon him when the British moved on Boston. It was said that Thomas's plans to defend Breed's Hill by quickly raising dirt and stone revetments turned the tide at the

Timeline

1941 1942-1945 1944

1941 – Duxbury Beach Association builds the pavilion at the public parking lot at the north end of the beach (Duxbury Beach Park).

1942-1945 – World War II. Duxbury Beach Association grants U.S. Army rights to use beach.

1944 – Hurricane destroys many trees and causes property damage on Clark's Island.

The Portland Gale

During the Portland Gale of 1898, Mr. Boardman, owner of the Gurnet Inn, had to go out to his barn on his hands and knees to care for his animals because of the force of the wild winds. A chimney blew down in the midst of the storm, and the stove had to be carried, fire and all, across the house to attach it to another chimney. Life was not for the faint-hearted in this remote and exposed spot.

famous battle of Bunker (Breed's Hill). Washington asked Thomas to stay in the army and sent him to Canada to retrieve some much-needed cannons. Sadly, he contracted smallpox and died on the way home.

Thomas left his entire estate to his wife Hannah, along with instructions as to how she should manage their affairs, including taking care of the lighthouse. Hannah, a determined woman with an independent streak, became the first female lighthouse keeper in America. According to the story, it was not without a struggle. Only after she told them to take their lighthouse off her land did the Commonwealth finally appoint her as keeper of the light. Having made her point, she hired Thomas Burgess to climb the frame towers every few hours, day in and day out, and insured herself for the sum of 500 pounds in case her stand-in did not perform properly. In 1790, the year that the newly established U.S. government took control of the lighthouse, Hannah's son John became the lighthouse keeper, serving until 1812.

The Gurnet Lighthouse has undergone numerous changes during its long history. A new lighthouse with twin towers was built in 1803 after a fire in

1801 completely destroyed the original building. The lighthouse was again rebuilt in 1843, this time as two octagonal towers joined by a covered walkway and set farther apart to give ships' crews a better view of the lights. In 1924, the north tower was removed, and the south tower was equipped with a flashing light of increased candle-power. The light was automated using solar power in 1986. The biggest change of all occurred in December 1998, when the U.S. Coast Guard moved the structure 140 feet back from the edge of the eroding 45-foot cliff to its present location against the north ramparts of Fort Andrew.

When the Gurnet light failed to keep ships from running aground or breaking up on the rocks, surfmen from the Lifesaving Service went into action. The first Gurnet Life-Saving Station, built in 1878, was replaced by a new structure in 1892. The fate of the original building is a typical example of Gurnet-Saquish thrift: it was carried off to Saquish, where it served as a boathouse until it was destroyed in the Portland Gale of 1898. The second Gurnet Life-Saving Station, which eventually became part of the U.S. Coast Guard along with the Gurnet Lighthouse, remained active until 1956. The building itself still stands proudly on the Gurnet headland as a private home.

At the base of the Gurnet headland, just before Saquish Beach, a one-room schoolhouse served the children of the surfmen, the light keepers, and the farm, as well as the children on Clark's Island, who rowed across the channel and walked along Saquish Beach to get to their little schoolhouse.

The Gurnet Lighthouse is supported on steel beams and wood cribbing, in the process of being moved to its new site.

1944-1945 – Pavilion at Duxbury Beach Park doesn't operate due to wartime gas rationing.

November 29, 1945 – Devastating storm essentially flattens beach.

1946 – Town of Duxbury proposes taking Duxbury Beach as a war memorial.

1947 – Waldo Herrick's last year of managing Duxbury Beach Park; parking fees increase from $0.25 to $0.50.

Timeline

1944-1945 1946 1947

At far right is the Gurnet Schoolhouse at the Saquish crossover, as shown in a drawing done in 1906 by H. Messinger Fisher. The inset shows a present-day cottage expanded from the original schoolhouse.

The Surfmen of the Gurnet Life-Saving Station

On July 31 of every year, the summer residents of the Gurnet celebrated the return of the lifesaving crew, or surfmen, to the Gurnet Life-Saving Station. The crew, which consisted of a captain and seven men, patrolled the shoreline from August 1 to June 1. When they spotted a ship in trouble, they shot flares into the air to alert the sailors that help was coming and to summon their fellow surfmen to respond quickly.

Rescue operations were carried out by lifeboat if possible or by a breeches buoy if the surf was too heavy for boats. The breeches buoy consisted of a ring buoy with a pair of canvas breeches (short pants) sewn into it. The ring buoy was suspended from a pulley attached to a long rope line. A surfman would shoot a line from the shore into the rigging of the ship, and one by one the sailors would climb into the contraption to be hauled to safety.

Life for surfmen meant constant lifesaving drills, routine housekeeping and maintenance duties, and long stretches of loneliness, punctuated by occasional acts of bravery and adrenalin-filled rescues. In 1892, the surfmen received $60 a month for their dangerous and skilled work. In that year, they had 19 rescues of ships small and large.

The men at the Life-Saving Station welcomed the summer residents of the Gurnet because their arrival marked the end of long months of winter isolation at the end of Duxbury Beach and the start of their own summer vacations.

Saquish Neck, the ephemeral sand spit connecting Saquish Head to the Gurnet, formed as sediments eroding from the Gurnet spread gradually westward until they reached Saquish. The lovely beach facing Plymouth is known as Crescent Beach for its concave shape. Once treasured for its clams, the beach now delights small children who find sand dollars in the shallow water.

The earliest dwelling on Saquish Head appears to have been what was fondly called the "old farmhouse." Photos of it before 1936 when it fell apart show it was a cape, probably started as a half cape, dating to the late 1600s or early 1700s. The foundation of this early dwelling is very interesting and mysterious. It is built of flat stones not found anywhere in the area. With the abundance of beach stones, one wonders why these stones were brought in from a distance.

Saquish

Saquish Head, variously spelled *Sagaquab, Sagaquis, Sagaquash, Saquaquash, Sasaquish*, and *Sauquish*, is an Indian word meaning "clams" or "place of many clams." Although Champlain showed it as an island in 1605, a 1774 map preserved in Pilgrim Hall, Plymouth, shows it connected to the Gurnet. In an oral history recorded in 1969, Captain Albert Franklin (Allie) Pierce, who was born in 1877 and became a seaman in the waning days of the great sailing ships, claims that Saquish was an island at high water until the Portland Gale in 1898.

1948 – Ralph Blakeman takes over management of Duxbury Beach Park, which comes to be known as "Blakeman's."

1949 – State attempts to take the beach.

1950 – Town begins to sell parking permits for $1 each to finance cost of policing resident parking lot.

1950 – State attempts to take the beach; 300 Duxbury residents attend hearing in Boston to voice opposition.

Timeline 1948 1949 1950

The foundation of the "old farmhouse" on Saquish Head shows a typical narrow profile similar to the Alden House foundation in Duxbury.

During the Civil War, when Fort Andrew was rebuilt on the Gurnet, a smaller fort was constructed on Saquish Head. Fort Standish had a gun mounted on each of its four corners and was manned by locals. After the war it fell idle, and a fisherman and his wife decided to use the underground lodging as their home. One evening when the wife went outside to call her husband for supper, the earthworks in the section collapsed, leaving them homeless but unhurt.

Although the old farmhouse has been connected with the Burgess family, who owned it from 1793 until 1902, the road past the house bears another name. Benjamin Hanks purchased the old farmhouse in 1742 and lived there for four years before leaving Saquish and moving west. Local lore posits that he is the same Benjamin Hanks whose granddaughter, Nancy Hanks, gave birth to Abraham Lincoln 63 years later. The main road across Saquish Head is named Hank's Avenue in honor of the family.

From the earliest habitation and into the twentieth century, the occupations of Saquish's few residents were fishing and farming, supplemented during Prohibition by a little rum-running. Nor were the settlers above accepting occasional gifts from the sea. As Captain Pierce recounted, "One winter, a vessel loaded with lumber went aground on Brown's Bank but was able to free itself and came into the inside cove of Saquish. Before the underwriters were able to come down, Hurley and Peiffer got enough lumber to build each of themselves a house."[3]

They Got Me Hooked on Lobstering

In 1945, my father built a small cottage on Saquish Head. Getting there in our old Model-A Ford was always an adventure, as we got stuck in the sand at least half a dozen times each trip. At that time Saquish was a small summer community with approximately 15 houses on the Head and only three houses on the sandy neck between Saquish and Gurnet. More important to me, it was also a seasonal fishing community.

My uncle Elija Eldridge spent each summer in the cottage we now own at Rocky Point. Uncle "Lige" and Aunt Dotty raised eight children in that little house. Uncle Lige was a lobsterman in the summer and moved to Dennis in the winter to harvest scallops.

Allie Pierce lived with his wife on the landing at Saquish. He was a lobsterman in the summer and a boat builder in Plymouth in the winter. His son Franky and family lived in the house next door. Franky was also a lobsterman.

Russ Harlow and his housekeeper Edna Lucas lived on the front side of Saquish Head. They lived in the main house and rented two cottages on the property in the summer. I spent a lot of time with "Uncle Russ" and "Aunt Edna." Russ was a big man and very stern, but he had a great sense of humor. Aunt Edna was a wonderful cook who loved children.

Like Allie, Russ was a lobsterman in the summer and a boat builder in the winter. He is the reason for my love of the sea. I lobstered with him a lot, as did Clint Watson. Clint would row over from Clark's Island at daybreak each morning. Russ would run his lobsters by boat to Plymouth once a week. He would take whoever wanted to go with him to stock up on provisions for the week.

When Russ retired from lobstering, he sold his boat to Bill Jacobs. Although Bill lived on the Gurnet, he kept his boat anchored in the more protected waters at Saquish and I continued to lobster with him. When I think of Saquish, I think of Uncle Lige, Allie, Russ, and Bill—they all got me hooked on lobstering.

Bill Bennett, Duxbury.

Russ Harlow, driving, with "Aunt Edna" and Walter Penniman.

1951 – Frederick T. Pratt succeeds his father, Frederick S. Pratt, as chairman of the Duxbury Beach Association.

1952 – Access road to Duxbury Beach is proposed across marshes of Back River.

Timeline 1951 1952

Barney's Gulf Station

Until four-wheel-drive vehicles became commonplace, many summer residents of the Gurnet, Saquish, and Saquish Head depended on ordinary cars to gain access to their cottages.

Traversing stretches of soft sand and beach rock out to Saquish in an older, two-wheel drive vehicle was quite a challenge. Standard equipment typically included a tripod jack, boards to place under the tires, and a shovel, as getting bogged down in the sand was very often part of the trip.

Drivers also had to remove some of the air from the tires to keep them from digging into the sand. This is where Barney's Gulf Station came in. Upon leaving the beach, Barney's was always the first stop—to put air back in the tires. Barney always had an air hose available and always had time to chat for a few minutes. Who can forget the sound of the bell on the air tower ringing off the pounds of air as the tires were filled?

Norman Forgit, Saquish Beach.

Saquish remained unchanged for many years owing to the difficulty of transportation and the legions of mosquitoes. Draining the pools where they bred reduced the numbers of mosquitoes, and the advent of the jeep after World War II accelerated the process of transforming Saquish into a summer colony by making the area easily accessible. Saquish Neck was the site of a veritable population explosion during the 1950s when about 50 cottages were built. Many cottages sprouted up on the Saquish and Gurnet headlands as well. Today there are 55 dwellings on the Gurnet, 120 on Saquish Beach, and 52 on Saquish Head. These houses have been passed down in families more often than sold.

Pulpit Rock, also known as Election Rock, is where the small party of men from the Mayflower *gave thanks on the Sabbath for their safe landing on Clark's Island two days earlier and "elected" to settle at Plymouth Bay.*

Clark's Island

The small size of Clark's Island—86 acres belies its importance as the site of the first religious service in New England. The story, often told, is worth repeating.

Leaving the *Mayflower* anchored off Provincetown on Wednesday, December 6, 1620, 18 men in a shallop (a small, open boat) ventured along the inside of Cape Cod, looking for a likely spot to settle. William Bradford, who described the events, was of the party. As they neared Plymouth Harbor on December 8,

> *it begane to snow & raine, & about ye midle of ye afternoone, ye wind increased, & ye sea became very rough, and they broake their ruder, & it was as much as 2 men could doe to steere her with a cupple of oares. But their pillott bad them be of good cheere, for he saw ye harbor; but ye storme increasing, & night drawing on, they bore what saile they could to gett in, while they could see. But herwith they broake their mast in 3 peeces, & their saill fell over bord, in a very grown sea, so as they had like to have been cast away..."*[4]

August 31, 1954 – Hurricane Carol damages the dunes and parts of the Powder Point Bridge. Roof blows off pavilion and walls are seriously weakened.

1959 – Town Meeting turns down a motion to provide $800 for beach patrols.

September 11, 1960 – Death of T. Waldo Herrick, first operator of Duxbury Beach Park.

Timeline 1954 1959 1960

Narrowly averting disaster on the rocks off Gurnet Point, they "rowed lustily" and managed to land safely on what turned out to be Clark's Island. The name came from the mate of the *Mayflower*, John Clark, who was supposedly the first person to step ashore. The next day the party spent drying their "stufe" and repairing the shallop, and the following day, being Sunday, they "prepared there to keepe ye Sabath."[5] Today the enormous rock on the island where they gave thanks, known alternately as Pulpit Rock or Election Rock, welcomes "pilgrims" at the Duxbury Rural and Historical Society's annual Clark's Island picnic.

The colonists established a pest house on Clark's Island for the care of any sick arrivals to the colony in order to prevent the spread of disease. Legend has it that a dedicated "Mother White" took care of these travelers until they could enter the little village of Plymouth. She sailed into the harbor twice a week to pick up provisions and exchange news but she was not allowed to land.

During King Phillips War, 1675–1676, the "praying Indians" in the colony (those who had converted to Christianity) were sent into exile on Clark's Island, partly for their own protection against their angry Native American brethren, but mostly because the colonists feared the converts might turn against them. In 1675, the Council of War ordered that the "Nemassachusett Indians be speedily removed to Clarkes Iland, and ther to remaine and not to depart from thence without lycence from authoritie upon paine of death."[6] With no provision for shelter or means of support, surely many must have perished, but history is silent on their fate.

The town of Plymouth sold Clark's Island to Samuel Lucas, Elkanah Watson, and George Morton in 1690. A short time later, Watson became the sole owner of the island, and on the cellar hole of the old pest house, he built his home. From that time on, the story of Clark's Island is intertwined with the story of Elkanah Watson and his descendants.

The first Watsons probably supported themselves initially by cutting trees, because many of the cedar posts used in

Oh, How I Love the Gurnet

My love affair with the Gurnet began over 70 years ago when good fortune brought my family to vacation there with their friends the Holmes. Each summer we rode over the beach in Bill Jacobs' old beach buggy, sitting on his lobster bait barrels. During World War II, no one was allowed on the Gurnet, and my parents discovered that the Cape provided an easier vacation with cottages that had electricity, indoor plumbing, and running water. I became increasingly homesick for the Gurnet and even wrote a nostalgic essay for my high school yearbook recalling the Gurnet's special magic.

After college, I decided to spend a few days with Mrs. Upham, the mother of my parents' friends. She owned the first cottage on the ocean side as you come onto the Gurnet. My plan was to get over my childhood crush on the place—but no, it was stronger than ever. When Mrs. Upham suggested that I buy the last lot of land she owned, I did. I then purchased a prefab building to put on it. What a thrill to stand at my front doorway as the sections were assembled and to have my own private view of the beach and sea. I learned to shingle and lay flooring, and many times I carried my tools and materials over the beach since I had no car.

Marriage and the birth of two sons fulfilled my dream of having children who would enjoy the Gurnet as I had as a child. We added on to the cottage, with the boys learning how to build at an early age. Later, my remarriage and the birth of another son (who made his first trip to the Gurnet when only a few weeks old) resulted in additional improvements to the cottage. We began to spend more and more time at the beach and only returned to our Duxbury house late in the fall. Finally, in 1980, we moved out to the Gurnet year-round. Being there every day was a thrill and still is!

In January 1987, we lost our home in a terrible fire that consumed everything we treasured and the place I had worked on all my adult life. It is still too painful to write about. But, like the Phoenix, we rose from the ashes, and with the now-skilled builders my sons had become and the know-how of a wonderful husband, we rebuilt. I decided God did not want a middle-aged lady to rest on her laurels. I realized I must get up and do it all over again—paint more paintings, take more photographs, and write more stories about the place I love.

The Gurnet has provided so much happiness for my family. It is where my sons and I have learned about the sea, about nature, and about the early inhabitants. I will always be grateful for having such a beautiful place to call home.

Elaine Nudd,
longtime resident of the Gurnet.

Timeline

1961 1962 1963

March 11, 1961 – Duxbury town meeting approves $4,500 for a beach patrol budget; Duxbury Beach Association agrees to provide a jeep for patrols.

June 17, 1962 – First volunteer beach cleanup

March 9, 1963 – Duxbury Town Meeting establishes Conservation Commission.

seventeenth-century Boston came from Clark's Island. Sassafras, an important crop used for medicine, also grew on the island. A salt works was operated by the Jenny family, relatives of the Jennys who had the grist mill in Plymouth.

One of the early Watsons owned a hay baler (a large press that flattened the stacks of hay), and thanks to this marvelous machine, the family began to prosper. Salt marsh hay cut on the Gurnet and Saquish was brought to Clark's Island, baled in the Watson's barn, and shipped to Plymouth to sell. An addition to the house, put on in 1740, testifies to their rising fortunes.

One of Elkanah Watson's descendents, also named Elkanah, was an ardent Tory. He owned several properties in addition to his Clark's Island property. However, as the tides of fortune changed, his properties were confiscated, and he was forced to leave the colony and relocate to Nova Scotia. His son, John Watson, who had sided with the patriots, became head of the family, which then withdrew to Clark's Island, about the only one of Elkanah's possessions that had not been taken from the family.

During the War of 1812, the Watsons were able to hire captured British sailors to build stone walls that still mark old boundaries on the island. In 1836, the Watsons built a second house, "Cedarfield," on the east side of the island. With prosperity came time for leisure. One famous visitor was Daniel Webster, who shared the Watsons' interest in agriculture. Edward Winslow Watson was a great friend of Webster, and the two of them experimented with raising exotic plants and trees.

Clark's Island was just the sort of place that would appeal to the transcendentalists, and indeed was visited by Henry David Thoreau, Ralph Waldo Emerson, and Louisa May Alcott. Alcott is reputed to have spent several summers in the main Watson house. In 1885, William Watson Goodwin, a professor of Greek at Harvard, built a house on the south end of the island, which became a gathering place for intellectuals in the summers.

The writers and intellectuals who stayed with various Watsons were not the only ones coming to Clark's Island. At the

Plymouth vs. Nathaniel Clark

Thomas Clark, no relation to John Clark, was a carpenter who reportedly arrived in Plymouth on the Ann in 1623. For many years he enjoyed the undeserved distinction of having been the first mate of the Mayflower, a myth that may have been perpetrated by his son Nathaniel in an attempt to gain possession of the island.

Nathaniel Clark was an attorney-at-law "or as near to one as the conditions and exigencies of the times either permitted or required" in the words of an unsympathetic writer. He was serving as Secretary of Plymouth Colony in 1686 when King James II sent Sir Edmund Andros to be governor of the Dominion of New England, a short-lived consolidation of several colonies, including Plymouth. Formation of the dominion abolished the separate colonial governments and thoroughly angered the colonists. Nathaniel Clark, out of a job, "fastened himself to the royal Governor, and became one of his most subservient instruments and tools."

When Governor Andros declared all public lands, including Clark's Island, to be property of the crown, Clark petitioned to have Clark's Island granted to himself. The written notice, signed by Andros, was read at the Plymouth town meeting on January 23, 1688. Despite widespread anger in the town, the petition was evidently successful because two months later a surveyor recorded that he had surveyed and laid out Clark's Island for Nathaniel Clark.

The town, however, did not give the island "to this usurper without resistance." A special town meeting was called to devise a plan to reclaim the island, a committee was chosen for the purpose, and subscriptions were collected to cover the costs of the undertaking. The government reacted by arresting various committee members "for levying . . . taxes upon his Majesty's subjects," and the case was bound over to the Supreme Court at Boston. These delays and obstructions only increased the spirit of resistance and strengthened the town's resolve to exercise its rights.

The matter had not yet been settled when King James was overthrown in 1688. The news reached Boston in the spring, whereupon a group of colonials seized and imprisoned James' hated royal governor. The new English rulers, William and Mary, ordered Andros and his subordinates, including Nathaniel Clark, to England to stand trial. At a town meeting, the inhabitants of Plymouth passed an official declaration against Clark, asserting that he "hath been a real enemy to the peace and prosperity of the people, . . . caused much trouble and damage, ...[and] endeavored to deprive us of our lands."

Clark's Island was restored to Plymouth, but in order to cover expenses incurred in the attempt to prevent the taking by Clark, the town voted to sell the island and other holdings, including Saquish and the Gurnet. In 1690, Clark's Island was sold to Samuel Lucas, Elkanah Watson, and George Morton.

Quotations are excerpted from W. T. Davis, **History of Plymouth County, Massachusetts with Biographical Sketches**, (Philadelphia, J. W. Lewis & Co., 1884).

Mid-1960s – Volunteers led by John Nash erect snow fencing to deter erosion and prevent vehicles from driving over dunes.

1966 – *Duxbury Clipper* prints ad: "Wanted, Dead or Alive," requesting tinsel-free Christmas trees for erosion control on Duxbury Beach.

1968 – Frederick S. Pratt, aged 95, resigns after 50 years as trustee of Duxbury Beach Association; Charles H. Wood replaces him.

Timeline

MID-1960s 1966 1968

end of the nineteenth century, a three-story boarding house with 17 rooms was built just south of the old Watson house, and among its guests were people who came for the excellent goose and duck hunting. There was a gunning stand at the north end of the island, where people hunted not just for sport but for market. Hundreds of fowl were shot and sent to Boston. Turnips grown on the island were packed with the birds, and "Clark's Island turnips" appeared on the menus of well-known restaurants such as the Parker House.

No place is perfect. James Watson, who built catboats on the island, was fatally shot on the island in 1898 and is buried under a black tombstone. The period of the two world wars brought depression and hard times to the island. The last year-round resident of Elkanah Watson's house left in 1927, swimming his cattle across to Saquish and then driving them down the beach. About this time, the island houses were becoming summer homes for a younger generation of Watsons.

After a hiatus of about 50 years, Clark's Island again found its niche as a center for the arts. Sarah Wingate Taylor, another Watson descendant, hosted a colony of poets at Cedarfield. Howard Watson, manager of public relations for the *Saturday Evening Post*, bought the house at the south end of the island and invited several authors, among them Truman Capote. Capote spent the summer of 1959 on the island and could sometimes be seen going to and from Duxbury seated in the back of a boat, wearing his signature long coat and hat.

In the 1970s, houses began to pass out of the Watson family. Today, of the 11 houses on the island, two belong to Watsons (Clint Watson and his brother David's children), and three, including Elkanah Watson's original estate, belong to Watson kin. Cedarfield has been given to the Duxbury Rural and Historical Society, and five houses have been sold outside the family, a trend that will likely continue because of soaring property values. Taxes reflecting the desirability of this prime waterfront land are putting a strain on the old families of Clark's Island, and Gurnet and Saquish as well. It is to be hoped that new owners will appreciate the history and traditions of these special places.

Sarah Wingate Taylor, the Poet of Clark's Island

Sarah Wingate Taylor (1906-1964) spent nearly all her summers on Clark's Island. Her ancestors, the Watsons, had owned the island since the 1690s. Each summer, her parents took her to Cedarfield, the island's second oldest house, built in 1836. There she came to love the island's history and the quiet beauty of its unspoiled fields and rocky shores. Eventually, she inherited nearly half of the island including Cedarfield and Election Rock, the site where a weary group of Pilgrims took shelter in 1620, observed their first Sabbath in the New World, and "elected" to settle at Plymouth Bay.

After a 10-year career as a free-lance journalist in 1930s Boston, Taylor was hired in 1945 by Dominican College in San Francisco to teach Shakespeare. Despite living across the continent, she still considered Clark's Island home and returned there each summer.

The island was a perfect environment, Taylor felt, to inspire creativity, and she was determined to share it with young scholars. Her first attempt at bringing bright minds to the island was a poet's colony, which she opened in 1937. In doing so, she continued the traditions of her great Uncle Edward Watson, a renaissance man who welcomed such great writers as Emerson and Thoreau to Clark's Island. Taylor had a gift for verse and published several volumes of poetry, most of it related to the island's history. Her poet's colony was successful, but closed in 1942 due to the war.

In 1963, she launched a more elaborate project, the Pilgrim Rock School of American Studies. The program consisted of a six-week session, during which students read and discussed classic works of New England literature in the island's tranquil setting. The school did well for two summers, but closed after Taylor's death in 1964.

Taylor's extended family donated her beloved Cedarfield and Election Rock to the Duxbury Rural and Historical Society in 1969. Each summer, the general public is invited to the island for an afternoon to reflect on its history and, ideally, to take with them a piece of the inspiration that Taylor so wished to share.

Patrick Browne, Executive Director,
Duxbury Rural &
Historical Society.

Timeline

1968

May 30, 1968 – Death of Frederick S. Pratt, founder, chairman, and trustee of Duxbury Beach Association.

1968 – Duxbury Beach Association sets aside land at High Pines to protect nesting least terns from disturbance, posting signs: "Terns Resting."

1969

1969 – Fiftieth anniversary of Duxbury Beach Association.

Gallery

The twin towers of the Gurnet Lighthouse and the bell tower (at far right), c. 1890. The surfmen of the Gurnet Life-Saving Station (shown below) rang the bell during rescue missions and sometimes during severe weather when wind would muffle the sound of the foghorn.

The original Life-Saving Station on the southwest side of Gurnet Point, c. 1890.

Left: *The north side of the farmhouse (the Boardman's inn) at the Gurnet, c. early 1900s. Chickens can be seen in the farmyard.*

Below: The boathouse, c. 1930. The surfmen would sometimes give the children a ride in the lifeboat before they began their drills.

Below: A summer afternoon at the Gurnet, c. 1880. The house in the center still exists. The original Life-Saving Station is at right, with Saquish Beach and Clark's Island in the distance. The Myles Standish Monument (under construction) can be seen on the horizon at far right.

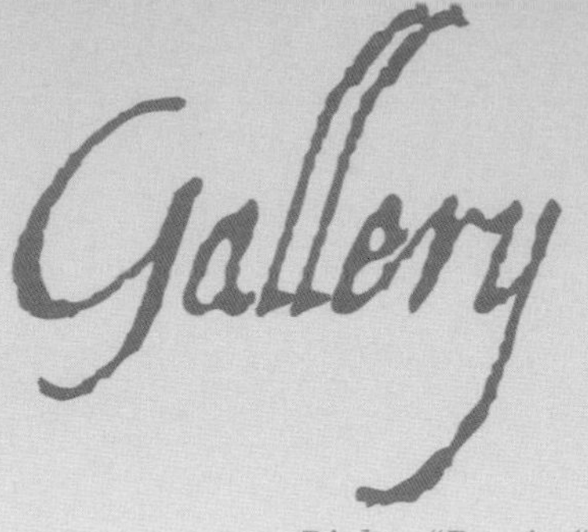

Right: "Bessie," one of the Gurnet's farmyard "residents," c. 1890. The barn burned in 1925.

Below: Visitors to the Boardman's inn, which they called the Gurnet Inn, arriving by horse and buggy, driven by Mr. Boardman, c. 1900.

The cover of a brochure promoting the inn, which the Boardmans operated from 1885 to 1905.

Above: Houses, cottages, and fishing shacks at the base of the Gurnet near the area known as the "boathole," c. 1900. The cottage in the center, long owned by the Richards family, is decorated, possibly for a Fourth of July celebration.

Right: Bill Jacobs, lobsterman and longtime resident of the Gurnet, knitting heads (nets) for his lobster traps, c. 1955.

Gallery

Right: Aerial view of the Gurnet, looking south, c.1940s. The lookout tower, constructed during World War II, can be seen at the top center, with the earthworks of Fort Andrew surrounding it.

Below: Looking north at the farmhouse, c.1900, showing the turnip crop, the farmhands, and the ox team.

These three photos, looking north at the cliff below the Gurnet Light, show the erosion that has occurred over a period of nearly 60 years. The top photo was taken in 1940, the middle photo in 1980, and the bottom photo in 1997, shortly before the lighthouse was moved back from the cliff.

Each year since 1929, the "Flying Santa" has flown either by plane or helicopter over the lighthouses of New England, dropping gifts for the lighthouse keepers and their families. Well-known author Edward Rowe Snow was one of the "Santas" for many years.

Gallery

Another photo of the houses and fishing shacks at the base of the Gurnet near the area known as the "boathole," c. 1880. This photo was made from a glass plate negative.

An early view of the Gurnet looking northeast, showing the boathole at far left, and the first Life-Saving Station just behind the house to the left of the sailboat, c. 1880. At the right of center is the original lighthouse keeper's house and the twin lights.

Moving Gurnet Lighthouse, 1998. At left is the new foundation for the light. Below is the light at its new site, 140 feet back from the eroding cliff.

The boathole at the base of the Gurnet, with the road out to Saquish in the distance, c. 1930s. The cottages in the center still exist, but the cottage at left was washed away during the Blizzard of '78.

Gallery

Tall ships visit Plymouth in 1992. Taken from Saquish Beach.

A cluster of houses on the Gurnet, c. 1937. The Life-Saving Station, with its rooftop lookout, and the boathouse can be seen on the far right.

A Norse spindle-whorl found on the Gurnet headland. It was used by Norse women to spin wool or flax onto a wooden spindle, with the stone wheel (whorl) at the bottom to keep it turning. This artifact is nearly identical to one pictured in the November 1964 issue of National Geographic Magazine.

Above: Saquish Beach in 1937, looking east toward Gurnet Point.

Right: An aerial view of Saquish Beach, looking north, with Duxbury Beach in background.

Gallery

Saquish Beach at low tide, with Gurnet Point in the background c. 1950.

Above: Saquish Head looking northeast, with Saquish Beach in the distance, taken from the area near the remains of Fort Standish, c. 1920.

Left: The old farmhouse at Saquish Head, c. 1920s.

Left: Plowing turnip fields on Clark's Island in the 1930s with a mule flanked by two horses. Below: Harvesting the turnips.

Bottom: Cedarfield on Clark's Island, c.1900. Sarah Wingate Taylor owned this 1836 cape for many years. Saquish can be seen in the background.

Gallery

Right: Aerial view of Clark's Island in 1946, looking north.

Below: A cyanotype print of Clark's Island looking east across Cedarfield toward Duxbury Beach, the Gurnet, and Saquish Neck, c.1890.

Right: The house on the west side of Clark's Island, c. 1880s.

Below: The William Watson Goodwin house at the south end of Clark's Island, c. 1900.

Removing scrap metal on Clark's Island for the war effort in 1943.

Gallery

Right: A poem written by Sarah Wingate Taylor in 1916, at the age of nine, along with a newspaper clipping showing the poem published.

Below left: Sarah Wingate Taylor arriving at Cedarfield with her belongings.

Below right: Sarah with her brother William Watson Taylor in the 1920s.

Here comes the tide
As it's blue waters rise and
go
with the sea gull flying
over head
As if it were their faith-
full guide.
Here comes the tide
As it's blue waters ris
and go.
and ~~As~~ my heart with t
beats
As ~~And~~ each morn
it repeats
e rythm of the
deeps
and we recall
the sad refr
he clashing of
the fleets.

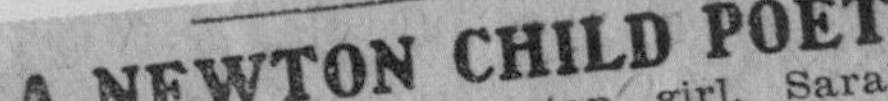

A NEWTON CHILD POET

A bright little Newton girl, Sarah Wingate Taylor, daughter of Mr. and Mrs. Harry M. Taylor, has written a number of verses that show remarkable talent and skill for a miss only 9 years old. Several of them have been printed in the local papers. Two are printed below:

THE TIDE

Here comes the tide,
As its blue waters rise and go,
With the sea gull flying overhead
As if it were their faithful guide.
Here comes the tide,
As its blue waters come and go;
And my heart with it beats,
As each morning it repeats
The rhythm of the deeps;
And we recall the sad refrain
Of the clashing of the fleets.

THE SOLDIER BRAVE

I'm a soldier brave and bold,
(As the story ran, I'm told),
See me pierce the paper through,
See me break the chair in two.
Here I climb up mountain stairs,
Here I'm riding on the chairs;
Here the pillows make retreat,
Here again in war I meet.
Hark! here comes nursie, stern but
kind,
With mother running close behind
To see what mischief they can find;
Now see the soldier brave and bold
Making fast for some stronghold;
Sure they'll catch me if I wait,
Knowing well my sad fate.

Right: The 1903 wedding of Elizabeth Villa Taylor to Albert Mortimer Watson. The reception was held at Cedarfield.

Below: The well on the island, taken in 1961.

Below right: A family gathering, taken at Pulpit Rock, c. 1910.

8 DUXBURY BEACH... The Living Beach

The Seasonal Nature of Wildlife

Barrier beaches that buffer the continent from the open ocean are vibrant and ever-changing landscapes. The land itself is in motion, bending and rolling to the energy of wind and surf and time. The Atlantic barrier beaches, like Duxbury Beach, are inundated with ephemeral wildlife as well as limited numbers of permanent residents. The beach is a rough place to make a living, but there are seasonal eruptions of wildlife that depend utterly on the beach. The horseshoe crabs come to the sandy edge to lay eggs annually, and the migrant shorebirds pass along the beach going to their nesting territories in the far north in perfect time to dine on the horseshoe crab eggs. The rare piping plovers arrive to nest on the beach, and the blue fish and striped bass arrive in their season as well. Other creatures also use the beach as a seasonal haven. These include the wintering snowy owls; the brant that graze on the underwater plants; and three species of scoters, two species of loons, and other sea and bay ducks that loll along the coast through the winter.

Sanderlings, often in loose flocks, are one of the few shorebirds that use the outer beach. They are most often seen in their pale "non-breeding" plumage.

Timeline

1969 – Family of Sarah Wingate Taylor donates Cedarfield and Election Rock to the Duxbury Rural and Historical Society.

1973 – Town meeting votes to lease the beach for $12,000 a year, and town hires W. Neal Merry as first beach conservation officer.

April 1973 – Richmond Poole and 27 of his students plant 15,000 culms (stalks) of American beach grass in one day.

The Snowy Owls' Winter Sojourn

Visitors to Duxbury Beach arrive each year from a variety of places, but few from anywhere as foreign or distant as the snowy owls. These hardy birds leave their Arctic breeding grounds in November to winter on our relatively balmy New England seacoast, making the long journey home again in February or March. Many of the migrating owls stop at Logan Airport, where Norman Smith traps and bands them. The FAA requires that he relocate the owls, so in the first half of the winter he releases them in Duxbury as if they were moving south. (An owl with a spot of color on its head is one of these Logan transplants.) In the second half of the winter he releases them north of Boston, as if they were migrating northward.

During the months they are among us, the snowy owls are wonderful to behold. While many owls are nocturnal, snowy owls are active daytime hunters—not surprising when you consider that they spend the summer months in the almost continuous daylight of the Arctic. The snow-white façade, which gives the owl its name, is another adaptation to life in the far north. A dense layer of down covered by thick feathering enables the owl to maintain an internal body temperature of 100 to 104 degrees in outside temperatures as low as minus 58 degrees Fahrenheit.

Perched on fence posts and standing 18 inches tall, these magnificent birds are the largest owls to visit or live in Massachusetts. To catch sight of a snowy owl is one of the great pleasures of the winter beach.

Based on article by John Day in ***Beach Soundings***, Newsletter of the Duxbury Beach Preservation Society, Vol. 6, No. 1, 2002.

The seasonal arrival of native people to harvest the returning fishes, to gather clams and mussels, or to trap migrant ducks and geese had little effect on the wildlife of the great marshes protected by the barrier beach. These animal populations existed in profusion, and the seasonal harvest had little impact on overall numbers. There were always young creatures to replace those that made their way to the fires and cook pots of the indigenous people. The bay was a place where a subsistence society could spend the warm months and be assured of food.

As the semi-nomadic people of previous centuries gave way to permanent residents, cultural uses of beach wildlife began to change. For early colonists the migrant ducks and geese were a welcome sight. Though fish, of all sorts and seasons, were caught and dried or salted and crops were husbanded and stored in cellars or hung to dry, it was the birds, passing by in the fall, that provided both fresh and preserved food for the winter. For later hunters, the migrant birds could be turned into cash if they were sent to the city restaurants.

By the early twentieth century, Duxbury Beach was a well-known gunning spot. There were gunning shacks along the bay side, and in the fall, the water would be dotted with strings of decoys and low-sitting duck boats camouflaged with marsh grass. The beach is now rarely shot over, but fishermen cast along the shore for the resurgent striped bass and later for warmer water blue fish. Clammers scrape away the muddy sand for the soft shells that live a few inches down, and the oystermen of this new century plant and grow their rough-shelled crop on ropes and nets pegged to the bottom. The beach environment continues to yield up its treasures. The wildlife still arrives. The numbers have changed from previous centuries, some dramatically, but there are still the pulses of life that show the system is working.

The cycles along the shore are miraculous. The horseshoe crabs are a good place to start. These armored creatures were laying eggs in the sands of beaches 300,000 years ago, long before the last ice age created our shoreline. To this day, they are still laying their eggs along the edge of the ocean during the high tides of May and early June. The eggs are buried in the sand by the tens of millions, hatching in about two weeks. The migrant birds know this, and they arrive from distant wintering spots just in time to feast on the largess of the crabs' inefficient parenting technique. The birds feed and fatten and then continue on to the north to nest in the tundra or the muskeg or on a mountain far away, carrying with them molecules and energy that originated in Duxbury Bay.

The adult horseshoe crabs will head back to deeper water to scuffle along the bottom looking for small shellfish to crush and eat. The hatchlings that survive will float in the water for a week or so before sinking to the floor of the bay and burrowing into the bottom. There they will molt and grow for about 10 years until the females join their sisters to lay eggs along the shoreline and begin the cycle anew.

The migrant shorebirds of the late summer and fall will include several species of plover: semipalmated, piping, and black-bellied. The occasional golden plover is always looked for in the short marsh grass. The sandpipers will include dunlin, ruddy turnstone, semipalmated and least

1975 – Duxbury Beach Association transfers ownership of the beach to Duxbury Beach Reservation, Inc., a Massachusetts non-profit corporation created for that purpose.

1978 – The Blizzard of '78 overwashes beach in several places and destroys three of the six houses north of the pavilion.

Timeline

1975

1978

sandpipers, red knots, sanderling, and both greater and lesser yellowlegs. The fall passage can also bring in whimbrel, killdeer, and the occasional buff-breasted sandpiper or Hudsonian godwit.

Birds that nest on the beach are few. The willet, which started nesting here in the 1980s, is a large gray shorebird that nests in the salt marsh vegetation. This rather drab-looking bird explodes into a black and white pattern when it rises in flight. The willet's loud and raucous call has become a regular part of a summer's day.

The piping plover is listed as threatened by both Massachusetts and the federal government. These small birds will return in late March or April. They scrape a shallow nest in the cobble (small stones) and lay four eggs. If all goes well, they incubate the eggs for five weeks and then wander with their hatched and precocious youngsters for another three weeks. After that, the chicks fledge (fly on their own). Often, high tides or predators will destroy the nests, and the birds will try to hatch a replacement clutch. This can lengthen the nesting season.

The piping plover is given the right-of-way by federal law, and beach goers, especially those in oversand vehicles, are quite restricted until the young can fly. The need for protection has prompted the Duxbury Beach Reservation, in cooperation with the town of Duxbury, to develop a management plan that monitors and protects each of the piping plover nests and limits and controls activities on the beach until the young fledge. This plan has allowed the beach to remain open and available to the public during the nesting season.

The least tern, although not considered threatened like the plover, is listed as a "species of concern" by the Massachusetts Natural Heritage and Endangered Species Program. This small bird is the least predictable of our nesting species. Least terns will appear and disappear, only to reappear during the early part of the summer. They will sometimes not establish a nesting site until mid-May or occasionally later. They will usually nest as a colony in an area of sand and cobble. The least tern is very visible and noisy as it rises up to harass and distract all creatures, great and small, that venture near the colony.

Clams, Mussels & Oysters: from Fine Food to Ashtrays

Over the years, several species of mollusks found in Duxbury Bay and along the beach have become an important part of the local diet and economy. No summer clambake is complete without soft-shelled clams, also known as steamers because of the way they are cooked. Steamers are raked out of the mud at low tide. Razor clams are long, narrow mollusks shaped like a barber's razor. They are found standing vertically in low tide flats, and are most often used to make chowder. Northern quahogs, hard-shelled clams that also are raked at low tide or stumbled across with bare feet, can go in chowder or be stuffed, although the mid-size cherrystone and smaller littleneck varieties are often served on the half shell or in pasta dishes. Two species of mussels—the ribbed and edible blue—are also commercially viable. Blue mussels form large colonies that attach themselves to pilings (like those supporting the bridge) and rocks, while ribbed mussels burrow into mud or peat.

On the ocean side, Atlantic surf clams sometimes roll up on the beach after a heavy surf, but they are usually caught on the ocean floor by dragger fishermen who sell them for use in commercial chowder. The surf clam's large shell with blue patches on the inside also makes it a popular ashtray at coastal restaurants and bars.

What you are more likely to find from Duxbury waters in a restaurant nowadays, however, are oysters. The wrinkled shell of the eastern oyster has become a Duxbury hallmark. They are farmed in the bay and shipped to gourmet restaurants around the country, where most oyster aficionados prefer to eat them raw.

There have never been many mammals on the beach. Herbivorous (plant-eating) mammals do not find enough food on a barrier beach, and the carnivores often depend on the herbivores. There have been occasional populations of red foxes, eastern cottontail rabbits, and striped skunks, and in the twentieth century both eastern coyote and raccoon have moved onto the beach. But aside from a steady, albeit modest, population of meadow voles and eastern cottontails, there are few resident mammals.

Marine mammals are rarely seen on Duxbury Beach. A few harbor seals will haul out in the winter on the rocks down by Gurnet, and an occasional one will

Timeline

1984

1985

1984 – Post and cable fencing of right-of-way is completed, defining a roadway from the bridge to the Gurnet.

May 14, 1985 – Ralph Blakeman retires after 38 years of managing Duxbury Beach Park. Gordon Leighton, who had worked with Blakeman for 14 years, takes over.

June 11, 1985 – Fire on Powder Point Bridge, believed to have started from a fisherman's lantern, causes severe damage.

Food for Flight

The beach is long and windswept and harbors few creatures year round. Some insect larvae feed on the beach vegetation in the summer, and other insects, like the monarch butterfly, use the flowers as a food source as they migrate past.

In the winter, life is quite slow on the beach. The plants produce seeds in large numbers, hoping that one or more of them will perpetuate the species. The seeds survive to feed the meadow voles that winter in modest numbers in the vegetated areas. These small mammals are what the snowy owl, the occasional northern harrier, and the ever-wandering eastern coyote look for in the short days of that cold season.

The shorebirds that we see during their spring and fall migrations rest at high tide, but when the tide goes out, they feed in wet or damp areas and on the exposed flats. They are looking for small animals, mostly amphipods, which live in the sand and mud. The beach will feed a migrating bird for up to a week, and then it flies off, turning the newly gained fat into energy to power the migration. In the winter there are a few dunlin and black-bellied plovers on the bay side and the occasional sanderling on the ocean side.

wander up on the sand. The harbor seals that are seen along the shoreline are a mix of adults and young animals, many three years old or less, and are wintering here, having arrived from the Canadian Maritimes. The larger gray seal and whales are rarely seen along this shore.

The wildlife of Duxbury Beach is not the same week to week or even day to day. The beach is especially exciting for the very fact that it changes season to season and day to day. For a naturalist, a walk on the beach is new and different each time. The only constant is the change and the feeling of contentment that change brings. Unto each thing there is a season and when we see those changes we can hope that all is right with the world.

A great egret at Gurnet Creek.

Least tern sheltering a chick.

The two main habitats of the beach are the upland dunes and the wet marshes. Each area has its own suite of plants and animals. Though the plants are present throughout the year, they are seasonal in their flowering and fruiting. Many of the animals that use the beach are migratory and are only present for a short period of time each year.

Gallery

The eastern coyote reentered eastern Massachusetts in the late 1980s after being extirpated in the early 1800s. Though most of them are mainly gray with red tones, this female was a beach resident for several years and was almost all sandy red.

The large gulls of Duxbury Beach (the herring and great black-backed) take four years to achieve their adult plumage. This young herring gull has caught a crab, but gulls are notoriously omnivorous.

Right: The animals present on the beach vary throughout the calendar year. The snowy owl is a northern visitor that uses the beach in the winter.

Above: Immature shorebirds migrate south a month or so after the adults arrive on Duxbury Beach from mid-August through late September. The semi-palmated sandpiper (left) and the red knot (right) eat, rest, and gain body fat to power their onward migration.

Left: The horseshoe crab is an ancient life form that continues to live along our shores. They can be seen in large numbers coming ashore to lay eggs on the spring high tides.

Gallery

During the year we see birds of different ages on Duxbury Beach. This young snowy owl (probably a female) is darkly barred.

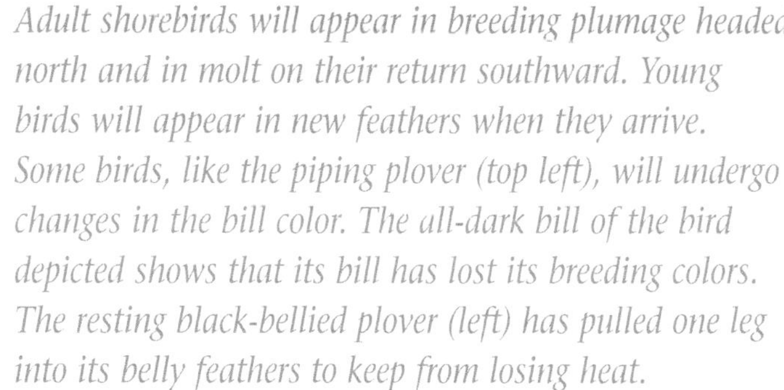

Adult shorebirds will appear in breeding plumage headed north and in molt on their return southward. Young birds will appear in new feathers when they arrive. Some birds, like the piping plover (top left), will undergo changes in the bill color. The all-dark bill of the bird depicted shows that its bill has lost its breeding colors. The resting black-bellied plover (left) has pulled one leg into its belly feathers to keep from losing heat.

Above: The great black-backed gull is the largest of North America's gulls. It is a rather recent arrival in the northeast but can be found throughout the year on Duxbury Beach.

Right: The brant is a small goose that nests on the low coastal tundra well to our north. This dark goose grazes on grasses, and similar vegetation, both on land and in the shallow water of our saltwater bays.

Gallery

The young harbor seals that make their way to our shores in the fall and winter originate well to our north. Generally the older seals stay in the northern waters, and the seals that we see are three years old or less.

In the winter the immaculate white head of the breeding herring gull turns a dusky and streaked gray. The gulls that nest on Clark's Island, both great black-backed and herring gulls, utilize the extensive flats in Duxbury Bay.

The ruddy turnstone walks the edge of the beach turning stones and shells, and digging into the sand, looking for worms and arthropods that are sheltered at, or near, the surface of the beach. In flight, the turnstone remains attractive with a flashing pattern of black, white, and red.

The huge colony of common terns that was located on the nearby Long Beach (Plymouth Beach) was abandoned due to the presence of predators. Common terns are now seen more often before and after nesting season. The numbers along Duxbury Beach peak in the late summer.

Gallery

The beach is a safe haven for coastal migrants. Among the less common shorebirds to use the beach in passage are the whimbrel (above) and the Hudsonian godwit (left). The whimbrel can be in the salt marshes or along the shore, and the godwit is usually moving in and out with the edge of the tidal water.

The dunlin is the most common of the winter sandpipers that use the beach. They are often in large flocks, and their long, somewhat drooping bill will confirm a winter identification.

The monarch butterfly's fall migration is coincidental with the flowering of the seaside goldenrod in the dunes and along the back road of the beach. The butterflies will stream past in the fall, consuming nectar from the flowers as they pass.

Gallery

Above: An adult piping plover is the color of the dry beach and is well camouflaged when nestled into the sand.

Three center photos: The nest of a piping plover is little more than a scrape in the sand. The eggs and the chicks are mottled so that they are difficult for predators to locate.

Left: "Exclosures" are erected around a piping plover egg clutch to protect them from predators like skunks, opossums, foxes, and crows. From the piping plovers' point of view, these might be called "enclosures."

These young least terns have taken shelter in an old whelk shell. Cold weather and driving winds force the young birds to seek shelter in anything from an old shell to a tire track.

The snowy owl hunts on silent wings. It feeds on small mammals as well as bay ducks. These owls hunt in the daytime as well as in the dark. Their summer breeding ground is the arctic, where there are often 20 or more hours of daylight each day, so they are used to daytime hunting.

Managing a Barrier Beach

Duxbury Beach Reservation, Inc.

Duxbury Beach Reservation, Inc., the current owner of the beach and successor to the Duxbury Beach Association, was organized on November 21, 1975, as a Massachusetts charitable corporation for the purpose of preserving the ecological value of the beach and making it available as a recreational resource for Duxbury residents and the general public. To ensure that these objectives are met, the Reservation's bylaws require that its governing body shall include representatives of environmental organizations and that a majority of the directors shall reside in Duxbury.

Three trustees of the former Duxbury Beach Association—Bartlett Bradley, Thomas Herrick, and Charles Wood—became directors of the Reservation, providing continuity between the old and new organizations. They were joined by Al Krahmer and John Nash, who had long been involved in volunteer efforts to stem erosion on the beach, and Robert Millar, whose wife's father, grandfather, and granduncle had all been trustees of the Association. Appropriately, Frederick T. Pratt was made Honorary Life Trustee.

Flood tide, Duxbury Beach, November 2003.

Timeline

1985

1986

July 23, 1985 – State inspects bridge repairs but finds additional weak points and closes bridge permanently.

1986 – Annual town meeting appropriates approximately $3 million for construction costs of new bridge.

1986 – Piping plovers are designated as a federally threatened species.

Duxbury Beach Reservation, Inc. Statement of Purpose

The purposes of the corporation shall be to acquire by purchase, gift or otherwise all or any part of Duxbury Beach and Saquish Beach in the towns of Duxbury, Marshfield and Plymouth and any salt marshes and upland adjacent to or in the vicinity of such beaches and also conservation easements or any other interest in or to any such property; to restore and to preserve these beaches (whether owned or not) in so far as reasonably possible in their natural state as host to marine life, native and migratory birds and indigenous vegetation, as barrier beaches for the protection of Duxbury and Kingston and as a priceless environmental asset to the Commonwealth and the nation; and to operate for the benefit of the people of Duxbury and the general public a public recreational beach with all necessary and incidental facilities, while preserving the right to limit and regulate such use so as to be consistent with the corporation's primary ecological objective.

Articles of Incorporation, 1975.

The Reservation followed in the footsteps of its predecessor, using income from Duxbury Beach Park operations, plus $12,000 from the annual town lease, to maintain and improve the dunes. In its first year of operation, the Reservation planted 12,000 culms (stalks) of beach grass with the help of volunteers, applied 12 tons of fertilizer, erected 1,000 feet of snow fence, and put up 5,600 feet of post and cable fencing along the right-of-way to the Gurnet. A major project was the relocation of 1,900 feet of the right-of-way just south of the bridge, made necessary by the gradual westward movement of the beach.

Another major undertaking initiated by the Reservation's directors in 1976 was the construction of the "Sandgrabber." Hollow cement blocks 3 feet high and 4 feet wide were strung together in a 200-foot arc in front of the pavilion at Duxbury Beach Park in an effort to trap sand and slow erosion. A northeaster shortly after installation shifted the blocks, but the tie-rods held and the structure continued to accumulate sand until it disintegrated in the Blizzard of '78. Like the sand catcher in 1933, the Sandgrabber was effective under normal conditions but unable to withstand the forces of a major storm, and by any definition the Blizzard of '78 was a major storm.

When the blizzard struck, the beach proved its value as a geological barrier for the protection of Duxbury and Kingston by saving those towns from the degree of destruction experienced by other oceanfront communities. There was serious damage on the beach, however. Most of the 8,000 culms of grass and 165 Rosa rugosa shrubs planted in 1977 washed away, along with much of the snow fence. In addition, three of the six cottages north of the pavilion were completely destroyed. Affirming their commitment to return the beach to as natural a state as possible, the directors of the Reservation voted not to renew the leases, in effect denying permission for the owners to rebuild the three cottages.

The blizzard prompted a greatly expanded program of annual maintenance. Instead of planting between 6,000 and 8,000 culms of beach grass as in the years prior to 1978, the norm now became 40,000 to 50,000 culms planted by conservation officers as well as volunteers. Snow fence

Robert G. Millar

Robert G. Millar, who helped to create Duxbury Beach Reservation in 1975, served as its treasurer and clerk for 12 years and often acted as president. He stepped down as director in 1987, continuing to provide wise counsel as a trustee until his death in 2004. What Frederick S. Pratt was to the Duxbury Beach Association, Bob Millar was to the Reservation. As his legacy, he collected, edited, and arranged all of the deeds, reports, letters, and newspaper clippings pertaining to the Association into ten bound volumes and the proceedings of the Reservation into four volumes. These he gave to the Duxbury Free Library. In recognition of his innumerable contributions, the Reservation established the Robert G. Millar Award in his honor in 1999.

Timeline

1987 1988

1987 – Duxbury Annual Town Meeting votes to create permanent Duxbury Beach Committee.

August 29, 1987 – New Powder Point Bridge officially opens.

1988 – Duxbury's Battelle Institute sponsors first annual international Coast Sweep Beach Cleanup to begin documenting beach debris.

American beach grass is used to re-vegetate beach areas. These plants, which thrive on wind-deposited sand, withstand heat, drought, and salinity. The sand they trap helps dunes recover after being battered by winter northeasterly winds and storms. With the help of volunteers, the Reservation plants thousands of culms of beach grass each spring.

went from 1,000 feet in 1976 to a yearly average of 15,000 feet after 1978. The Reservation continued the job, begun by the Association, of fencing both sides of the right-of-way to reduce the number of crossovers to the front beach and to confine traffic to a single track on the bay side of the dunes. Each year as much post and cable fencing was added as the budget would allow until demarcation of the right-of-way was finally completed in 1984. The deeded right-of-way was now a defined roadway along the entire length of the beach.

This expanded program was made possible by higher revenues from public parking at Duxbury Beach Park and an increased lease payment from the town, which was itself receiving more revenue from beach permit sales—nearly $120,000 in 1984 compared with about $50,000 in 1980. The Reservation raised the town's lease payment to $15,000 in 1984, arguing that it was only fair for the town to assume a larger share of the increased beach maintenance costs.

For the most part, the 1980s were a time of optimism for the Reservation. Its annual reports from the decade are full of such comments as, "Rebuilding of the dunes and growth of beach grass

The Duxbury Beach Preservation Society

As the Reservation struggled to repair the beach following the devastating No-Name Storm of 1991, it soon became apparent that its finances were woefully inadequate for the task at hand. At the same time, many residents and non-residents alike were offering to help with the restoration effort. A group emerged and named itself the Save Duxbury Beach Committee. The volunteers offered beach grass and snow fencing certificates, T-shirts, and beach towels in recognition of donations to the Reservation. They also sponsored a beach walk and a huge outdoor benefit dance. The group had to continue its fund-raising activities in the wake of another severe northeaster that flattened the original artificial dune and required construction of a second dune. The public response to "Save Duxbury Beach" was overwhelming and much appreciated by the Reservation.

Once the beach was finally put back together, the Reservation began to discuss how to continue restoration efforts, replenish the storm damage fund, and begin long-range planning. Thus was born the Duxbury Beach Preservation Society, a subcommittee of the Duxbury Beach Reservation, Inc., in 1995.

The Preservation Society has a twofold mission: to raise funds for beach preservation projects and the storm damage fund and to educate the public about the importance of taking care of the beach. Its motto is "saving our beach for future generations." Membership in the Preservation Society is open to all.

since the 1978 storm have proven dramatically the effectiveness of the dune restoration program," and "Each year the beach is better able to withstand a severe storm." Money from the Reservation's reserve for storm damage was occasionally spent, but overall the fund was growing.

In contrast to the 1980s, the 1990s will be remembered as the time when a combination of devastating storms and complex new regulations rendered management of Duxbury Beach much more difficult and costly. The No-Name Storm hit on October 30, 1991, sweeping away sand, fence, and grass—all the successes of the 1980s—and two of the remaining cottages. As the Reservation directors worked to repair the damage, they faced a shortage of both sand and money. Seawalls and jetties in adjacent coastal communities had blocked off the natural supply of sand, effectively starving

Timeline

1991

1992

October 30-31, 1991 – No-Name, Halloween, or Perfect Storm overwashes entire beach.

May 1992 – Save Duxbury Beach Committee forms to raise money to repair beach.

1992 – First "sacrificial dune" is constructed on Duxbury Beach to repair damage from No-Name storm.

Record Fledge Rates

The Reservation first began actively protecting piping plovers in 1993. Now each nest is monitored from 7 A.M. until 8 P.M. each day until the chicks fledge, or learn to fly. In 1996, Duxbury Beach achieved a record of 2.9 piping plover chicks fledged per nest and consistently has one of the highest fledge rates in the state. In 2006, 15 nests yielded 20 fledged chicks, or 1.33 fledges per pair, which is above the 1.25 fledges per pair required to sustain the species. Without the monitoring program, which is financed by the Reservation and administered by the town's harbormaster, most of the beach would be closed for recreational use during late spring and summer.

the beach and making it necessary to import sand from inland quarries for dune repair. The Reservation's storm damage reserve was totally inadequate for the work required.

Following emergency repairs made in the aftermath of the No-Name Storm, Al Krahmer, the Reservation's vice president in charge of operations, undertook the daunting task of constructing a so-called sacrificial dune, 16 feet high, and 10 feet wide at the top, down the entire length of the beach. Although FEMA agreed to pay 75 percent of the more than $1 million cost, the Reservation had to pay the bills first, then wait months for reimbursement. This it did by taking a $200,000 loan and asking for donations—two firsts for the Reservation. In addition to the lease payment, now $20,000, the town agreed to cover the Reservation's projected shortfall of $95,000 for the sacrificial dune project.

The sacrificial dune was designed to withstand a "five-year storm"—that is, one that would be expected to occur on average once every five years. However, in December 1992, a powerful northeaster again flattened the beach, washing the new dune, grass, and fence out onto the marshes. Krahmer once again directed the building of a new dune, this one farther back from the ocean and thus farther from the reach of waves. To make room for the dune, the roadway had to be moved and rebuilt farther to the west. Once more FEMA agreed to cover 75 percent of the $1 million plus cost for these projects, and once more Reservation Treasurer John Leonard struggled to pay the bills until FEMA's reimbursement checks arrived.

Accomplishing the two dune projects required navigating a maze of regulations administered by the Conservation Commission, the Department of Environmental Protection, the Natural Heritage and Endangered Species Program, the U.S. Fish and Wildlife Service, and the U.S. Army Corps of Engineers. To obtain all the necessary authorizations, James G. Kelso, the Reservation's vice-president for environmental permitting, filled out countless forms and spent hours in complex negotiations. In the process, he learned that new laws were beginning to require that restoration work not interrupt the natural, landward migration of barrier beaches. This had implications for the management techniques used on Duxbury Beach.

The traditional, instinctive response to washovers and blowouts had been to push the sand back up off the marshes to form a wall against the sea, but coastal geologists were advising that a lower, flatter dune profile would sustain less damage by letting the waves roll over the beach. Today's regulations require that

Please, Plovers, Nest on the Bay Side

In 1999, the Reservation undertook an experiment to create "replicated habitat" on the bay side of the beach in an attempt to entice piping plovers to nest away from the ocean side where they are at greater risk from storm waves and human recreation activities. A grassy area 150 by 300 feet was covered with quarry sand to create an artificial habitat attractive to plovers. The first pair of piping plovers to nest that year chose the replicated habitat. Four smaller areas were created over the next two years, for a total of five. Although these replicated habitat areas were initially successful, they were expensive to build and filled in with grass surprisingly quickly. Attempts to clear the areas of grass by rototilling failed to restore suitable nesting habitat, but burning the grass has shown some promise. The Reservation continues to study ways to create and maintain replicated habitat.

Timeline

1992 – Volunteers plant 500,000 culms of beach grass on new dune.

December 1992 – A northeaster flattens newly constructed sacrificial dune.

1994 – A second "sacrificial dune" is built on Duxbury Beach.

1994 – Volunteers plant 300,000 culms of beach grass in "herringbone" pattern to facilitate passage of threatened piping plovers to the wrack line where they feed.

1992 1994

any material washed onto the marsh be left there, and that any sand and rock deposited in the parking lots can no longer be returned to the front, or ocean side, of the beach but must be cleared toward the west, even onto the marshes. Whereas in the past a new row of snow fence would be placed 8 to 12 feet east of and parallel to the previous year's fence, now the fence must be moved westward to conform to the eroding scarp, or face, of the dune.

The Endangered Species Act also brought about changes in beach management during the 1990s. Kelso was the first to become aware of its potential impact on Duxbury Beach, and his warnings led the Reservation to take a proactive stance by hiring monitors to protect nesting piping plovers, listed as threatened under the federal act. There was only one pair of plovers on the beach in 1990. In 1993, three pairs nested under the care of the first monitors. By the end of the 1990s an endangered species officer and a large staff of monitors were watching 12 to 14 pairs of plovers each season, protecting nests with wire cages, and deterring foxes with vials of coyote urine.

Besides hiring monitors to protect the nesting plovers, the Reservation also modified its grass planting program to reflect natural processes. While grass is important to stabilize the dunes, plovers need bare, unvegetated areas where their predators cannot hide. This is why washover fans, created when storm waves crash against the dunes and spread sand over the back beach and marsh, form ideal nesting habitat. The Reservation now plants grass and shrubs only in locations determined in collaboration with scientists from the Natural Heritage and Endangered Species Program.

After the No-Name Storm, the Reservation received permission to plant circles of grass 20 feet in diameter on the bay side of the dunes, leaving 20 feet between the circles. However, this technique left straight paths for wind to scour away the sand between the circles. The Reservation therefore negotiated the right to plant grass in a zig-zag, or herringbone, pattern. Each "bone" was 20 feet wide with

Doesn't the Town Own the Beach?

The fact that the beach is privately owned by the Duxbury Beach Reservation is obscured by the close working relationship the Reservation has with the town, so much so that when large projects take place, it is not unusual to overhear someone remark, "I don't remember voting for all this at Town Meeting." Although the Reservation provides the materials, equipment, and manpower to maintain and repair the dunes and parking areas, the town's role is more visible. Beach goers buy their beach stickers from the town; uniformed town employees greet them at the east end of the bridge; and official vehicles, some donated by the Reservation, all bear the town seal. The important point is not who owns the beach but rather the spirit of cooperation with which the town and the Reservation carry out their respective roles.

Who Pays for What?

The Reservation has no employees. It receives revenues from a portion of the parking receipts from the public lot at the north end of the beach, the town's lease payment, and donations. The operator of the pavilion at Duxbury Beach Park (under contract with the Reservation) receives a percentage of the public parking fees and all of the food revenue. All permit fees for the resident parking lot, as well as for resident and non-resident oversand vehicle permits, accrue to the town. These fees, not property taxes, pay for the beach lease and all other expenses the town incurrs in operating the beach.

The lease payment to the Reservation, initiated at $12,000 in 1973, has grown to $400,000. The town's income from parking sticker fees has also risen exponentially from $3,078 in 1964 to more than $1,500,000 in the most recent fiscal year.

20 feet of bare sand on either side. The herring bone pattern, which remained clearly visible for years, left open areas for birds while effectively trapping sand and building dunes. The most recent state grass planting guidelines allow grass to be planted in all areas of new sand, but culms of grass must be spaced 3 feet apart instead of 6 inches as was formerly done. Regardless of the pattern employed, grass planting is still an annual event, with volunteers of all ages doing much of the work.

Finally, the 1990s saw changes in the management of traffic on the beach. Oversand recreational vehicles (ORVs) became much more tightly controlled, with traffic down the beach allowed only on the designated roadway and only within posted speed limits. The number of crossovers to the ocean side was reduced to two, with a third crossover

1995 – Save Duxbury Beach Committee evolves into Duxbury Beach Preservation Society, a permanent subcommittee of the Duxbury Beach Reservation.

1998 – Duxbury Beach Reservation consultants insert eight stainless steel rods, at key points along the beach to monitor long-term and seasonal changes in barrier beach morphology.

Timeline

1995

1998

A Special Place

At the annual spring grass planting, experienced planters teach the newcomers, who are soon teaching other newcomers. A warm spirit of camaraderie compensates for the hard work and usually raw weather. Most of the volunteers come from Duxbury or neighboring towns, but several years ago a young girl surprised everyone by announcing she was from a town far inland. Asked why she had come so far to plant grass, she replied that Duxbury Beach was very special to her family. Not only did her grandmother and grandfather meet on Duxbury Beach on the Fourth of July, but also her mother and father—and on the Fourth of July! When the exclamations died down, she concluded, "and you can just bet where I'm going to be on the Fourth of July!"

south of High Pines available for emergency access only. On the beach itself, where vehicles used to travel anywhere at any speed, the harbormaster instituted an "established track" program in 1992, whereby ORVs must travel in a single track east of the dunes, parallel to the water's edge. They must park east of the track, perpendicular to the ocean, forming a barrier between moving vehicles and people enjoying the shore.

Besides confining vehicles to the improved right-of-way and established track, the town and the Reservation agreed to allow a maximum of 500 ORVs on the beach at any one time—fewer when tides are unusually high or threatened or endangered species are present. In recent years, the town has further refined this restriction by specifying a maximum of 250 resident and 250 non-resident ORVs. The 50-50 split is consistent with the Reservation's commitment to allowing beach access to town residents and the public alike.

Since its incorporation in 1975, the Reservation has taken its mission very seriously. To maintain a barrier against the sea, it has added sand to the beach in two dune projects and numerous repairs, then stabilized the new sand with fencing and beach grass. To preserve the natural heritage of the beach, it has developed comprehensive programs to protect vegetation and wildlife. To operate a public recreational beach within the confines of these ecological objectives, as well as state and federal regulations, the Reservation has always relied on the cooperation of beach goers and the assistance of the town.

It has been almost 90 years since Frederick S. Pratt raised the money to buy the beach and protect it for the common good. The grand experiment he set in motion—a very public "private" beach—is still going strong. Now, as Duxbury Beach continues its inexorable march landward, the Reservation's threefold challenge is to preserve and restore the beach in a manner consistent with what nature intended, to balance fairly the needs of beach goers and threatened species, and to have enough funds in reserve for the next big storm.

Remembering Barney

E. A. Bernard, better known and loved as "Barney," operated a gas station on St. George Street from 1938 to 1988—the same gas station where people returning from a weekend at the Gurnet or Saquish would stop to refill their tires with air, maybe fill up on gas, and certainly let the children run in for Barney's penny candy.

Barney loved Duxbury Beach and spent many quiet hours in the small parking lot next to the harbormaster shack. After he retired, he used to walk around the lot to exercise his two new knees, and then he would sit down to rest and watch what was going on in the bay. After he passed away in 2003, the Duxbury Beach Reservation was surprised and deeply touched on learning that, besides bequests to the Duxbury Education Foundation and the Partridge Scholarship Fund, Barney had left the Reservation a large sum of money.

The Reservation decided to acknowledge Barney's generous gift by placing a flagpole at his favorite spot. Granite blocks surround the pole so others can sit and enjoy the same view.

1998 – U.S. Coastguard moves Gurnet Lighthouse 140 feet back from eroding cliff.

2002 – BARC (Beach Access Rights Committee) forms to protest proposed dog ban on Duxbury Beach during plover nesting and breeding season; committee's efforts result in dogs being allowed if owner has permit and leashes dog.

Gallery

Aerial views of Duxbury Beach.

Below: Looking northwest, with the Powder Point Bridge at left, and Green Harbor and Brant Rock at right.

Right: Looking southeast, with Duxbury Beach Park at left, the bridge at right, and the Gurnet, Saquish and Clark's Island in the distance.

Gallery

Below: Looking southeast, with the bridge at bottom, and Duxbury Beach stretching off into the distance, ending at Gurnet Point.

Right: Looking northwest at Gurnet Point, with Saquish and Clark's Island in the distance.

Who's Who
on Duxbury Beach

The five original trustees of Duxbury Beach Association, serving from its inception in 1919:

William L. Benedict

Winthrop Coffin

Frank R. Maxwell

William Hill Young, *Secretary/Treasurer*

Frederick S. Pratt, *Chairman*

In 1934, Mr. Maxwell died, and Mr. Benedict asked to resign. Benedict's son, Dr. Edward B. Benedict, and Mr. Eben H. Ellison were chosen as their successors. Winthrop Coffin died in 1938. He was not replaced for several years, and the Association functioned with only the remaining four trustees.

In 1945, Dr. Edward B. Benedict resigned, and Frederick T. Pratt, the son of Frederick S. Pratt, was appointed. The Association continued to function with four trustees until, in 1952, Messrs. Harry B. Bradley and Thomas W. Herrick, Jr. became the first year-round residents of Duxbury selected to serve as trustees.

Eben H. Ellison resigned, making again a total of five trustees. Harry B. Bradley died in 1953 and was replaced by his son, Bartlett B. Bradley. William H. Young, who had served as secretary and treasurer since 1919, died in 1960. William P. Ellison, the son of Eben Ellison, was appointed trustee, and Frederick T. Pratt, who had acted as chairman since 1950, took on the role of secretary-treasurer as well. Frederick S. Pratt continued as trustee until 1968 when he was replaced by Charles H. Wood.

The trustees who worked out the transfer to Duxbury Beach Reservation, Inc. were Frederick T. Pratt, Thomas W. Herrick, Jr., Bartlett B. Bradley, William P. Ellison, and Charles H. Wood. On December 30, 1975, Pratt and Ellison, both of whom were shareholders, resigned to avoid any appearance of a conflict of interest. Herrick, Bradley, and Wood appointed Charles A. Krahmer a trustee, and they dissolved Duxbury Beach Association effective May 1, 1976.

Duxbury Beach Association Original Shareholders

To raise the purchase price of the beach, the following summer residents of Duxbury bought shares for $100 per share:

Frederick S. Pratt	20 shares,	$2,000
William L.Benedict	20 shares,	2,000
Winthrop Coffin	20 shares,	2,000
Horace H. Soule	10 shares,	1,000
William H. Young	10 shares,	1,000
Kate R. Winch	6 shares,	600
Clifton H. Dwinnell	5 shares,	500
Philip R. Allen	5 shares,	500
Sidney Harwood	5 shares,	500
Kenneth Hutchens	5 shares,	500
Howard D. Brewer	10 shares,	1,000
George P. Fogg	2 shares,	200
Jesse E. Donald	1 share,	100
Eben H. Ellison	10 shares,	1,000
Estate of Edward E. Elms	10 shares,	1,000
Frank R. Maxwell	5 shares,	500
John C. Runkle	1 share,	100
Frank L. Young	5 shares,	500
	150 shares,	$15,000

Looking south along Duxbury Beach.

Donors of the Beach

When the beach was transferred from the Association to the Reservation in 1975, there were 239 shares outstanding:

Helen Abbott	10
Laura Benedict (Anna Millar's mother)	9
Henry Bothfeld	9
N. Rust Cutler	1
William P. Ellison	25
Anne Runkle Hose	2
Albert Pratt	52-2/3
Frederick T. Pratt	52-2/3
Henry N. Pratt	52-2/3
Harriet E. Rogers	25

Shares were valued at $525 based on the liquid assets of the Association divided by the 239 shares. Those assets were transferred to the Reservation and used to buy out the shareholders. The beach itself, appraised at $1,116,000, was given to the Reservation.

Recipients of the Robert G. Millar Award, May 13, 2006, from left to right: Walter Amory, Charles A. Krahmer, Charles H. Fargo, John B. Nash, John P. Leonard, and Robert F. Hayes.

Original Members of Duxbury Beach Reservation

In November 1975, Edmund A. Dondero, Charles H. Fargo, John Nash, Roger Moore, and Charles H. Wood filed articles of organization for Duxbury Beach Reservation, Inc. with the Secretary of State.

The first directors of Duxbury Beach Reservation, elected at a special meeting held March 27, 1976, were, with their designations:

Dr. Lansing H. Bennett, *Trustee and Director, Duxbury Conservation Commission*

Bartlett B. Bradley, *Trustee and Director, Duxbury Resident*

Laurence Channing, *Trustee and Director, The Trustees of Reservations*

Charles H. Fargo, *Trustee and Director, Massachusetts Audubon Society*

W. Thomas Herrick, Jr., *Trustee and Director, Duxbury Rural and Historical Society*

Charles A. (Al) Krahmer, *Trustee and Director, Duxbury Resident*

Roger Moore, *Trustee and Director, Gurnet Saquish Landowner*

Charles H. Wood, *Trustee and Director, Powder Point Resident*

Edmund A. Dondero, *Director ex officio, Chairman of Duxbury Board of Selectmen*

John Nash, *Trustee*

Frederick T. Pratt, *Honorary Life Trustee.*

Map of Duxbury Beach, the Gurnet, Saquish, & Clark's Island

Landmarks and points of interest throughout
The Duxbury Beach Book *can be found on this map,*
based on the NOAA Chart of Plymouth Bay.

Officers of Duxbury Beach Reservation

The first officers of the Reservation were Bartlett Bradley, President; Thomas Herrick, Vice President; and Robert Millar, Treasurer/Clerk. They, together with Al Krahmer and Charles Wood, comprised the 5-member executive committee. Krahmer joined Herrick as a vice president in 1979, and after 33 years of service to the Association and the Reservation, Herrick stepped down in 1985. After 34 years of service, Bradley was succeeded as president in 1987 by Charles Fargo. Millar stepped down the same year and was replaced by two men: John Leonard as treasurer, and Robert Hayes as clerk.

While Fargo, Leonard, and Hayes continued to serve respectively as president, treasurer, and clerk for the next 18 years, there were several changes in the ranks of vice president. A second vice president, James Kelso, joined Krahmer in 1991, and in 1993, their Herculean efforts on the two sacrificial dune projects complete, they were succeeded by Walter Amory and Lester Smith. Smith was the Reservation's first coastal geologist. In 1998 they were joined by Alan C. Vautrinot, Jr. as a third vice president.

In 2004, Walter Amory turned over beach operations to Shawn Dahlen; James F. O'Connell, another coastal geologist, replaced Lester Smith; and Margaret Kearney joined the executive committee as a vice president.

A watershed moment for the Reservation was in 2006: Charlie Fargo, John Leonard, and Bob Hayes, who had run the Reservation through good times and bad since 1987, all resigned as officers and stepped down as directors. With Shawn Dahlen, Jim O'Connell, and Al Vautrinot remaining as vice presidents, Margaret Kearney became the third president, Clark Hinkley the third treasurer, and Peter Alpert the third clerk in the history of the Reservation.

Present Members of Duxbury Beach Reservation

Margaret Kearney, President, Director, and Trustee

Shawn Dahlen, Vice President, Director, and Trustee

James F. O'Connell, Vice President, Director, and Trustee

Alan C. Vautrinot, Jr., Vice President, Director, and Trustee

Clark J. Hinkley, Treasurer, Director, and Trustee

Peter A. Alpert, Clerk, Director, and Trustee

Kay Foster, Director and Trustee

William Hartigan, Director and Trustee

Noreen Wenger, Director and Trustee

Richard M. Whitney, Director and Trustee

Chairman, Duxbury Board of Selectmen, Director

Walter Amory, Trustee

Dorothy Baker, Trustee

Donald C. Beers, Trustee

Nancy Bennett, Trustee

Colleen Brayer, Trustee

Stephen H. Carleton, Trustee

John M. Carnuccio, Trustee

Joseph Conway, Trustee

Doug Dondero, Trustee

Deborah Drinkwater, Trustee

Charles H. Fargo, Trustee

Joseph M. Grady, Jr., Trustee

Donald Gunster, Trustee

Anita Haffey, Trustee

Robert F. Hayes, Trustee

Walter D. Keleher, Jr., Trustee

James R. Kent, Trustee

Charles A. Krahmer, Trustee

Edward F. Lawson, Trustee

John P. Leonard, Trustee

Michael P. McLaughlin, Trustee

Deborah Meyers, Trustee

John B. Nash, Trustee

Elaine Nudd, Trustee

W. Richmond Poole, Trustee

Lester Smith, Trustee

Joan Sundstrom, Trustee

Friend Weiler, Trustee

Jason Wolfson, Trustee

Officers of Duxbury Beach Preservation Society

(A subcommittee of the Duxbury Beach Reservation, Inc.)

Anita Haffey
Margaret Kearney
Joan Sundstrom
Noreen Wenger
Joseph Conway
Debborah Drinkwater
Nancy Bennett
Colleen Brayer
Andra Carleton
Donald Gunster
Nancy Krahmer
Michael P. McLaughlin
Pamela Schiller
John Sibley
Richard Whitney
Jason Wolfson

Powder Point Bridge Committee

(Established by Board of Selectmen, October 1985)

Abdul Hamedah
Neil Johnson
Gerald Kriegal
Margaret Kearney
Gilbert Burns, town engineer (ex-officio)

Members of Duxbury Beach Committee

The selectmen have appointed many "Duxbury Beach Committees" over the years to study particular concerns relative to the beach.
In 1987, annual town meeting voted to establish a permanent beach committee, comprising three designees from the Duxbury Beach Reservation, Inc.; three members from the town (later increased to six); and the Conservation Administrator, Harbormaster, and Chief of Police, ex-officio.

In 2007, committee members included the following:

Joe Conway, Walter "Terry" Keleher,
and Mike McLaughlin from the Reservation;

Dan Baker, William Benjes, Skip Bennett,
Colleen Carroll, Sarah McCormick,
and Susanna Sheehan from the town;

Dr. Thomas Gill representing the
Conservation Commission,
Mike Pforr representing the Harbormaster/Coastal
Natural Resources Department,
and a designee of the police chief.

Endnotes & Bibliography

Chapter 1

Bibliography

N. E. Chute, Geologic Map of the Duxbury Quadrangle, Plymouth County, Mass., 1965.

D. M. Fitzgerald, I. V. Buynevich, and P.S. Rosen, "Geological Evidence of Former Tidal Inlets along a Retrograding Barrier: Duxbury Beach, Massachusetts," *Journal of Coastal Research*, Special Issue 34, ICS 2000, New Zealand.

M. C. Hill and D. M. Fitzgerald, "Evolution and Holocene Stratigraphy of Plymouth, Kingston and Duxbury Bays, Massachusetts," in C. Fletcher, and J. Wehmiller, eds, Quaternary Coasts of the U.S.; Marine and Lacustrine Systems, S.E.P.M., Special Publication, 48, 1992, pp. 45-66.

M. C. Hill, D. M. Fitzgerald, and C. T. Baldwin, "Development and Assessment of Sand Resources in Plymouth Bay, Massachusetts," Technical Report No. 1, Marine Research Group, Department of Geology, Boston University, 1989.

J. F. O'Connell, "Shoreline Change Analysis, Mid-1800s to 1994, Duxbury Beach, Massachusetts," based on data from the Massachusetts Shoreline Change Project: 1800s to 1994, Technical Report and Maps, E.R. Thieler, J. F. O'Connell, and C.A. Schupp, U.S.G.S. Administrative Report generated in collaboration with the Woods Hole Oceanographic Institute Sea Grant Program and Cape Cod Cooperative Extension to the Massachusetts Office of Coastal Zone Management, 2001.

Chapter 2

Endnotes

1. Quoted from John Hay and Peter Farb, *The Atlantic Shore* (Harper & Row, 1966), p. 18.
2. *Mourt's Relation: A Journal of the Pilgrims at Plymouth*, Ed. Dwight B. Heath, (Cambridge and Boston: Applewood Books/Plimoth Plantation, 1986), p. 84.
3. William Wood, *New England's Prospect*, Ed. Alden T. Vaughn (Amherst, Mass.: University of Massachusetts Press, 1977), p. 56.
4. *Mourt's Relation*, p. 84.
5. Wood, pp. 50-51.
6. John Josselyn, *Colonial Traveler: Two Voyages to New England*, Ed. Paul J. Lindholdt (Hanover and London: University Press of New England, 1988), p. 73.
7. Wood, p. 52.
8. John Josselyn, *New-Englands Rarities Discovered* (Bedford, Mass. Applewood Press, originally published in 1672), pp. 6-7.
9. Josselyn, *New-Englands Rarities*, p. 3.
10. Josselyn, *Colonial Traveler*, p. 61
11. Ibid., pp. 87-88.
12. Wood, p. 37.
13. Justin Winsor, *History of the Town of Duxbury, Massachusetts* (Boston: Crosby & Nichols, 1849), p. 28.

Chapter 3

Endnotes

1. Memorandum and Extracts re Duxbury Beach Title, 1714-1832, Index to Records of Duxbury Beach Association and Duxbury Beach Reservation, pp. 87 ff.
2. "Life in Duxbury—1840" by Pauline Winsor Wilkinson, original 1921 manuscript in collections of Duxbury Rural and Historical Society, reprinted in the Duxbury Clipper Anniversary Issue, May 8, 1975, Section A., p. 8.
3. Duxbury Town Report, 1890, p. 36.

Chapter 4

Endnote

1. "An Act to Incorporate the Gurnet Bridge Company, and to Authorize the Building of a Bridge from Powder Point to Salter's Beach in the Town of Duxbury," Acts and Resolves of Massachusetts—1887, Chapter 301, Sec. 2.

Chapter 5

Endnote

1. Pages 65-72 are adapted from Susie and Bob Burnham, "The Perfect Storm: On Duxbury Beach," *Beach Soundings*, Newsletter of the Duxbury Beach Preservation Society, 4 (1), Fall 2000.

Chapter 6

Endnotes

1. "Duxbury Beach Association Trust Agreement, November 3, 1919," Duxbury Beach Association, Vol. 1., p. 56. Recorded at Plymouth County Registry of Deeds, Book 1351, p. 96.

2. Deeds for Sale of Pine Point Lots, Duxbury Beach Association, Vol. 8, pp. 238 ff.
3. Frederick S. Pratt, "Report of Chairman to Trustees, January 2, 1942," Duxbury Beach Association, Vol. 2, p. 316.
4. Ibid., January 3, 1946, Duxbury Beach Association, Vol. 2, p. 405.
5. "Duxbury Beach Appraisal, R.M. Bradley & Co., Inc., 1975-1976," Duxbury Beach Association, Vol. 6, pp. 216 ff.

Chapter 7

Endnotes

1. Samuel Adams Drake, *Nooks and Corners of the New England Coast* (New York: Harper and Brothers, Publishers, 1875), p. 269.
2. Charles W. E. Morris, "The Gurnet," *Pilgrim Society Notes*, 1 (30), Plymouth, Massachusetts, July 1982.
3. Albert Franklin Pierce, "A History of the Gurnet, Saquish, and Clark's Island, *Pilgrim Society Notes*, 1 (30), Plymouth, Massachusetts, pp. 2ff.
4. Wiliam Bradford, Of Plimoth Plantation, Manuscript journal written between 1630 and 1637.
5. Ibid.
6. Plymouth Colony Records, Vol. 5, February 29, 1676, p. 187.

Chapter 9

Bibliography

Duxbury Beach Association, Vol. 1.

Duxbury Beach Reservation, Inc., Vols. I-IV.

Duxbury Beach Reservation, Inc., Minutes of Duxbury Beach Reservation, Inc., 1987-1995, Vol. V.

Duxbury Beach Reservation, Inc., Records of Duxbury Beach Reservation, Inc., 1987-2005, Vols. VI-XII.

All of the above records are available in the Duxbury Room of the Duxbury Free Library.

Index

Designed and produced by Norman R. Forgit, Hanson, Massachusetts.

The typefaces used were Allegheny and Papyrus for headlines, and Stone Serif for body copy and captions.

Printed & bound by Worzalla Publishing Company, Stevens Point, Wisconsin

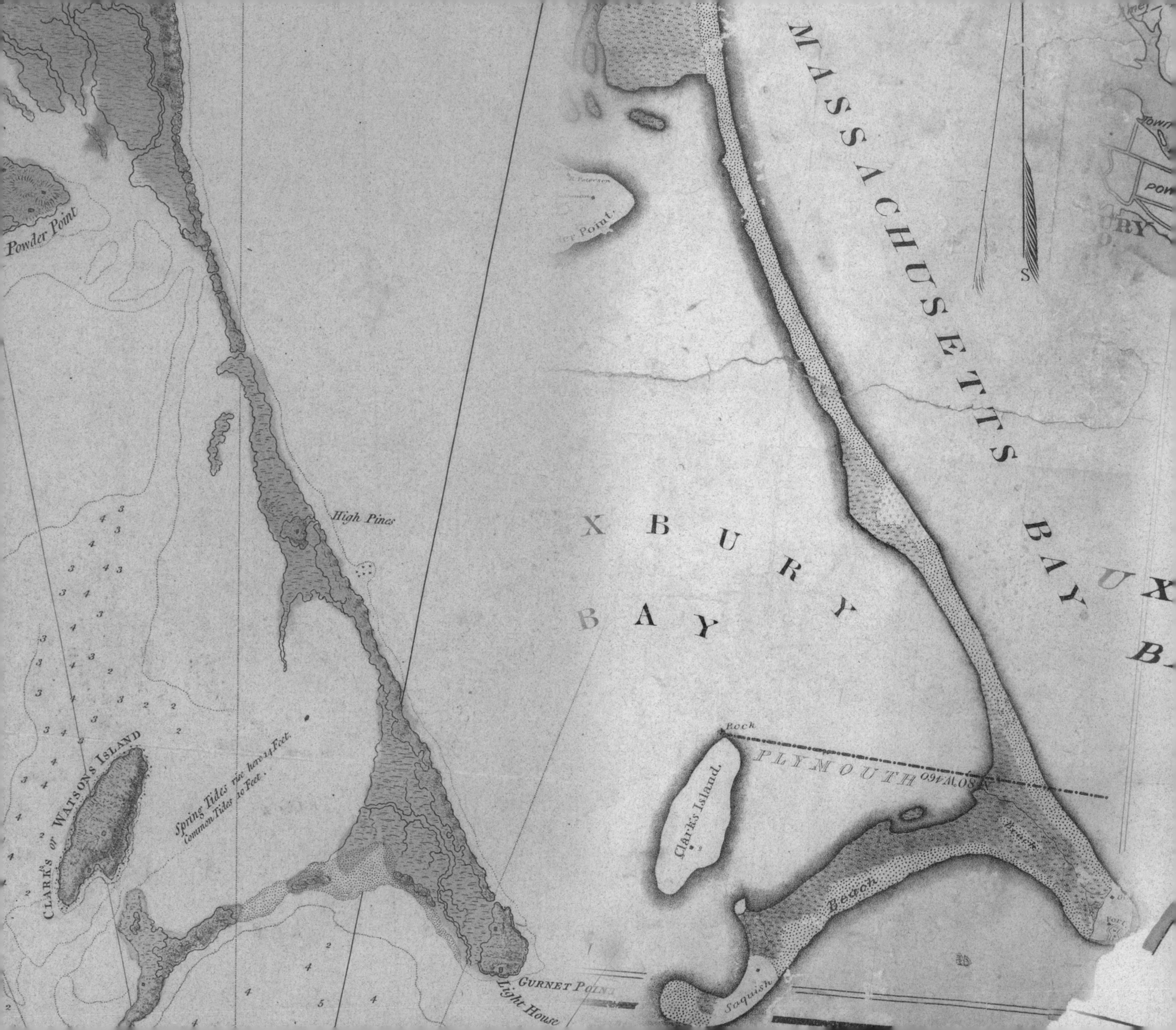

Powder Point
High Pines
MASSACHUSETTS BAY
XBURY
BAY
CLARK'S or WATSONS ISLAND
Spring Tides rise here 14 Feet.
Common Tides 10 Feet.
Rock
PLYMOUTH
Clark's Island.
Beach
Saquish
GURNET POINT
Light House